INTER-CHURCH RELATIONS:

Developments and Perspectives

A Tribute to Bishop Anthony Farquhar

Edited by Brendan Leahy

VERITAS

Published 2008 by
Veritas Publications
7/8 Lower Abbey Street
Dublin 1
Ireland

Email publications@veritas.ie
Website www.veritas.ie

ISBN 978-1-84730-095-9

Lines from *Two Sisters in the Spirit: Thérèse of Lisieux and Elizabeth of the Trinity* appear courtesy of Ignatius Press.

10 9 8 7 6 5 4 3 2

A catalogue record for this book is available from the British Library.

Designed by Lir Mac Cárthaigh
Printed in Ireland by ColourBooks Ltd.

Veritas books are printed on paper made from the wood pulp of managed forests. For every tree felled, at least one tree is planted, thereby renewing natural resources.

CONTENTS

Perspectives

CONTRIBUTORS' PROFILES

Seán Brady is Cardinal Archbishop of Armagh, Primate of All Ireland, President of the Irish Episcopal Conference and Co-Chair of the Irish Inter-Church Meeting. He has represented the Episcopal Conference at a number of Synods of Bishops held in Rome. As Archbishop of Armagh he has championed the cause of peace and worked energetically with the leaders of the other Christian denominations in challenging sectarianism.

Gerard Clifford is auxiliary Bishop of Armagh. He is a member of the Bishops' Commission for Ecumenism, the Advisory Committee on Ecumenism and the Inter-Church Standing Committee on Mixed Marriages. He is also a member of the Irish Inter-Church Committee (Ballymascanlon Conference) and the Episcopal Commission for Missions.

Mario Conti is Archbishop of Glasgow and an honorary Professor of Theology in Aberdeen University. He is a member of the Pontifical Council for the Promotion of Christian Unity and a Knight Commander of the Equestrian Order of the Holy Sepulchre of Jerusalem.

Adrian Cristea, born in Romania, is the Project Officer for the Parish-Based Integration Programme established by the Inter-Church Committee on Social Issues in 2007. Formerly Settlement Officer with the Vincentian Refugee Centre, he is on the Steering Group for the Anti-Racism, Diversity and Integration Strategy for Dublin City.

Tony Davidson has been Minister in First Presbyterian Church, Armagh since 1994, having previously ministered in Christ Church (united Presbyterian and Methodist) in Limerick. He is a former chair of ECONI (Evangelical Contribution on Northern Ireland). He is currently the President of the Irish Council of Churches.

7

Ray Davey is a Presbyterian minister. He was a prisoner of war just outside Dresden when it was firebombed in February 1945. He became Presbyterian Chaplain at Queen's University, Belfast in 1946 and founded the Corrymeela Community in 1965.

Michael Earle was born in Birmingham. He is General Secretary of the Irish Council of Churches and Executive Secretary of the Irish Inter-Church Meeting. He was formerly General Secretary for the Conference of Churches in Aotearoa New Zealand (CCANZ).

Susan Gately is a freelance journalist and news editor with Catholic Ireland News (cinews). A graduate of law and member of the Focolare movement, she attended both the Third Ecumenical Assembly in Sibiu and the 'Together for Europe' gathering of ecumenical movements in May 2007.

Crispian Hollis, formerly chaplain to Catholic students at the University of Oxford, has been Bishop of Portsmouth since 1988. He is currently Chairman of the Department of International Affairs in the Bishops' Conference of England and Wales. Previously, he chaired the Department for Mission and Unity.

Walter Kasper is Cardinal President of the Pontifical Council for Promoting Christian Unity. He is also a member of the Congregation for the Doctrine of the Faith and of the International Theological Commission. Formerly, he taught dogmatic theology and was dean of the theological faculty in Münster and later in Tübingen, Germany. He is author of numerous publications.

Gillian Kingston is a Methodist local preacher. She has been a member of the Methodist–Roman Catholic International Commission for some twenty years and is the immediate past president of the Irish Council of Churches. She has also served as Moderator of the Council of Churches Together in Britain and Ireland.

Brendan Leahy is Professor of Systematic Theology at St Patrick's College, Maynooth. He is secretary to the Bishops' Conference Advisory Committee on Ecumenism and member of the Inter-Church Standing Committee. Author of *The Marian Profile in the Ecclesiology of Hans Urs von Balthasar* (London, New City, 2000), he co-edited *Vatican II: Facing the 21st Century: Historical and Theological Perspectives* (Dublin: Veritas, 2006).

Thomas Norris is Associate Professor of Systematic Theology at St Patrick's College, Maynooth. A member of the International Theological Commission since 1998, he has written extensively on Cardinal John Henry Newman. His most recent publications are *A Fractured Relationship: Faith and the Crisis of Culture* (Dublin: Veritas, 2007) and *Living a Spirituality of Communion* (Dublin: Columba, 2008).

John Cecil McCullough is an ordained minister of the Presbyterian Church in Ireland. He has lectured widely and was Professor of New Testament in Beirut, Lebanon and Dunedin, New Zealand. Since 1988 he has been New Testament Professor in Union Theological College, Belfast.

Godfrey O'Donnell, born in Derry, is Assistant Priest of the Romanian Orthodox Church of the Exaltation of the Holy Cross in Christ Church, Leeson Park, Dublin. He has worked as a psychotherapist for many years. He is currently Chairman of the Dublin Council of Churches.

David Poole is a member of the Religious Society of Friends Meeting in Eustace Street, Dublin and former Clerk of their Ireland Yearly Meeting. He is a member of the Steering Committee of the Irish School of Ecumenics Trust and the Executive Committee of the Irish Council of Churches.

Sam Poyntz was Bishop of Cork, Cloyne and Ross (1978–1987) and Bishop of Connor (1987–1995). Bishop Poyntz was Chairman of the Irish Council of Churches (1986–1988) and Vice President of the British Council of Churches (1986–1990). He led an Irish Delegation to the first European Ecumenical Youth Conference in Lausanne, Switzerland in 1990, and subsequently other delegations to USSR and Israel/Palestine. During his time as Connor episcopate, he worked tirelessly for the marginalised in Belfast and especially the Shankill Road.

David Stevens is a Presbyterian lay person. He was General Secretary of the Irish Council of Churches from 1992–2003. Since 2004 he has been Leader of the Corrymeela Community. He is author of *The Land of Unlikeness: Explorations into Reconciliation* (Dublin: Columba Press, 2004).

John A. Radano has worked in the Pontifical Council for Promoting Christian Unity since 1984, where he is responsible for international contacts and dialogue with the World Alliance of Reformed Churches, the Baptist World Alliance and the Mennonite World Conference. He has also participated in dialogues with the Lutheran World Federation, Classical Pentecostals, the World Evangelical Alliance and the World Council of Churches. He has been a member of the Continuation Committee of the Global Christian Forum.

Eda Sagarra was born in Dublin and studied history and German at UCD, Freiburg and Vienna. She is professor of German at Trinity College and pro-chancellor of Dublin University. She was the founding chairperson of the Irish Research Council for the Humanities and Social Sciences. She has been involved in the School of Ecumenics since 1981.

Mary Tanner, a Dame Commander of the British Empire, is General Secretary of the Church of England's Council for Christian Unity and one of the Presidents of the World Council of Churches. She was Moderator of the Faith and Order Commission of the World Council of Churches from 1991–1998. She has also been a member of the Anglican–Roman Catholic International Commission.

Foreword

Cardinal Seán Brady

The search for unity and communion among the followers of Christ is of primary importance. For this reason, the Catholic Church's commitment to ecumenism is 'irrevocable'. Last November, at the consistory in Rome, I was able to see first hand just how much prominence Pope Benedict gives to this topic. Inter-Church relations were the main item on the agenda for the day-long reflection that preceded the consistory.

We know that Pope Benedict has followed with interest the promising political developments on this island and has encouraged every effort we can make to strengthen our bonds of communion and fellowship between the Churches. Thankfully, such relations are developing constantly. On the one hand, the official ecumenical landscape is now quite well established: there is the inter-Church meeting, annual ecumenical conferences, clergy and lay inter-Church fora and a wide range of initiatives at local and regional levels.

Before becoming Archbishop of Armagh and even more since then, I have admired Bishop Tony Farquhar's contribution to building up inter-Church relations. For some twenty-five years now he has engaged actively as a bishop in promoting bonds of friendship and understanding at times when it has been far from easy to do so. Grateful families on both sides of the 'divide', which he visited with gracious words of consolation during the Troubles regarding the deaths of loved ones, are but one example of the extent of his outreach in these years.

At the Bishops' Conference I have appreciated Bishop Farquhar's wise insights and advice, distilled from years of ecumenical experience, stretching right back to his time as university chaplain and his contact with the Rev. Ray Davey. His ability to see a humorous side to things and communicate joy, as well as his wide range of ecumenical knowledge and realism, has been much appreciated.

A hidden dimension of Bishop Farquhar's ministry has been his considerable commitment to international ecumenical dialogue. Typical of his self-deprecation, he has managed, without fanfare, to combine being Chairman of the Commission and Advisory Committee on Ecumenism of the Irish Bishops' Conference with the Co-Chairmanship of the Roman Catholic Church's Dialogue with the World Alliance of Reformed Churches, as well as being a member of the International Anglican Roman Catholic Commission for Unity and Mission. His achievement in overseeing the continuing Catholic–Reformed dialogue has been praised, not least because it is a dialogue that has been taking place during moments of tension in ecumenical relations.

I am very pleased, therefore, that this publication, *Inter-Church Relations: Developments and Perspectives*, has been put together in his honour. It brings together information and perspectives, updates and contemporary reflection from bishops, scholars and practitioners, all of whom have come into contact in one way or another with Bishop Farquhar's work in this area.

We need to be reminded continuously that inter-Church relations are developing. New things are happening all the time at both official and local levels. There is always room for further reflection and openness to perspectives 'from the other end of the pitch', as Bishop Farquhar would put it.

Any consideration of inter-Church relations brings us back to the radical source of all evangelisation, namely 'the encounter with an event, a person, which gives life a new horizon and a decisive direction'.[1] The truth is that 'love is now no longer a mere "command"; it is the response to the gift of love with which God draws near to us'.[2] It is this love that ultimately urges us to keep on working towards greater and improved inter-Church relations at all levels. This also means working together in 'the promotion of justice through efforts to bring about openness of mind ... to the demands of the common good'.[3]

It is concern for the common good that drives the Churches to contribute to both lasting peace and reconciliation in Northern Ireland and renewed Gospel commitment in response to the vast socio-cultural changes throughout the island. We live in an era of transition and with it there is a growing yearning for inter-dependence at all levels. Christians claim to go to God together. We need above all to witness, therefore, to our interdependence and mutual belonging as members of the Body of Christ. I hope the readers of this publication will be helped, as they strive in their commitment to foster ever improving inter-Church relations, to hear anew what today 'the Spirit is saying to the Churches' (cf. Rev 2:7).

Notes

1. Pope Benedict XVI, *Deus Caritas Est*, n. 1, *Acta Apostolicae Sedis* XCVIII (2006), pp. 804–815.
2. Ibid.
3. *Deus Caritas Est*, n. 28

Inter-Church Relations: Developments and Perspectives An Introduction

Rev. Prof. Brendan Leahy

W hy are there divisions among Christians? To this question many answers could be offered, but in his book, *Crossing the Threshold of Hope*, Pope John Paul II pointed us in an important direction. He wrote that perhaps such divisions have been permitted by God as 'a path continually leading the Church to discover the untold wealth contained in Christ's Gospel'. Indeed, maybe 'all this wealth would not have come to light otherwise'.[1]

It is true that the Churches have been thinking and acting in a plurality of ways that have led to different insights, traditions and expressions. This can be a source of contrast and tension but also of mutual enrichment. This book, written in honour of Bishop Anthony Farquhar on the occasion of his twenty-fifth anniversary of Episcopal ordination, strives to be a forum where we can listen to updates, insights and perspectives from different traditions and so be enriched.

The good news of recent times is that ministers and members of different Churches are more comfortable in recognising the wealth in each other's Church tradition and experience. As we strive together to best prepare for the gift of the ultimate visible unity of the Church, such recognition is important because it's a sign of the new outlook and new attitude that are always needed for healthy inter-Church relations. It facilitates 'a real re-reception of the same old truths in an ever-changing context' that will surely pave the way to greater unity.[2] It leads to what Pope Benedict calls 'concrete gestures that enter hearts and stir consciences,' inspiring in everyone that 'inner conversion that is the prerequisite for all ecumenical progress.'[3]

Such re-reception requires that Christians immerse themselves again and again in the always greater gospel that is transmitted in each generation through contemplation and study, as well as through the penetrating understanding of spiritual realities experienced along with the ministerial preaching of our communities.[4] The fact is that the words of the gospel are unique, universal and for all times. There's always more to discover, and we help one another in this discovery as together we exchange our spiritual, ecclesial and doctrinal insights.

To know one another (including our Churches and spiritual traditions) we need to love one another. To love one another we need to know one another. This interaction of knowledge and love in ecumenical dialogue has its requirements: 'Love is always patient and kind ... never boastful or conceited ... delights in the truth' (1 Cor 13:4–6). It is in listening to one another, in attentiveness to the voice of the Spirit for what is truly Christian in one another's words and insights, that we come to a 'deeper realisation of the mystery of Christ and the Church'.[5]

This collection of essays seeks to provide an opportunity where one of the first steps in ecumenical dialogue can take place, namely, the effort to allow ourselves and our communities to be drawn into the 'completely interior spiritual space in which Christ, by the power of the Spirit, leads us all, without exception, to examine ourselves before the Father and to ask ourselves whether we have been faithful to his plan for the Church.'[6] It seeks something of that dialogue of conversion to which we are all called.

The Ecumenical Glass is Half Full not Half Empty

Despite real differences and difficulties between Churches, the ecumenical glass is half full and not half empty. The commitment to good ecumenical contact is increasing, with stronger relationships

15

being built up at both official and local levels. A myriad of ecumenical events now form part of the annual calendar of the Churches, to the point that they hardly make news any longer – but that is good news.

On an international level, it is important to recall just how revolutionary the statement on justification is in terms of theological and devotional culture, to which Catholics, Lutherans and Methodists have signed up.[7] The Seattle Statement, *Mary: Grace and Hope in Christ,* proposed by ARCIC (Anglican–Roman Catholic International Commission), is also very significant.[8] These texts, detailing some of the central pillars of divisions between Churches, would have been unthinkable until relatively recently.

On this island, in the past year, a few significant steps in inter-Church relations have been noted. In Dublin, for instance, the Catholic Church has become a full member of the Dublin Council of Churches. In a statement on that occasion, Archbishop Diarmuid Martin noted that 'at a time in which many claim that ecumenical dialogue has encountered a slowdown, this decision of all the Member Churches of the Dublin Council is a sign of the vitality and the warmth of inter-Church relationships at the local level throughout the diocese'.

In the new Adamstown town centre in west Dublin, the Catholic Church, the Church of Ireland, the Presbyterian Church and the Methodist Church are to share one place of worship. This is the fruit of many years of solid ecumenical engagement between the Churches in that region.

While the Church of Ireland and the Methodist Church in Ireland continue to work in the light of the Covenant for greater cooperation and potential ultimate unity signed in 2002, the World Methodist Conference added its signature in 2006 to the Joint Declaration on the Doctrine of Justification by the Roman Catholic and World Lutheran Federation.

Improved inter-Church relations are not an optional extra, if for no other reason than, as Andrew Pierce has written, 'Irish Christianity makes its presence felt ecclesiastically, much more so than philosophically or ideologically' and that 'the deeds ... of the Churches will invariably impact on the credibility of the Christian witness in Irish society.'[9]

A Time for New Directions

Inter-Church developments in Ireland do not take place in a vacuum. Political events are so often in the background. New impetus for inter-Church relations also comes after the historic progress made in 2007 in Northern Ireland, a year described by President Mary McAleese as one of 'new directions, a new sense of purpose, new relationships, new friendships.'[10]

A sign of new directions could be seen, for instance, on Holy Thursday 2008, when Queen Elizabeth attended the Royal Maundy Service in St Patrick's Church of Ireland Cathedral, Armagh, distributing the Maundy money. It was the first time that the annual service was held in Northern Ireland. All of the main Churches in Northern Ireland were represented. Cardinal Seán Brady read the second lesson. Just over a month later, President Mary McAleese became the first President of Ireland to attend the Church of Ireland Synod, again with representatives of different Churches present as guests.

Just as the Churches played a very important role in promoting peace and reconciliation during the past forty years by witnessing to greater efforts at inter-Church contact and action, so too they continue to be key players in the search for new directions on this island. Scott Appleby in his book, *The Ambivalence of the Sacred,* contends that it is precisely when they 'remain religious actors,' and not by marginalising their beliefs,[11] that religious people continue to play a positive role in the world of human conflicts and contribute to peace. Whatever direction can and needs to be pursued by state agencies and other programmes, John Paul Lederach's observation holds true that something more than 'social technology' is required.[12]

What might this 'something more' be? Christians believe in an art of living according to the gospel. It is always to be proposed anew. The 'something more' that the Churches can offer flows from the heart of a renewed common commitment to *koinonia,* communion and fellowship in following Our Lord and Saviour, Jesus Christ – the gospel personified. This involves a new attentiveness to what has been called 'the studied practice of fraternity'.[13]

The demographic developments in the Republic of Ireland also prompt a new common sense of purpose. According to the latest

Census results, the Republic of Ireland's population is now made up of 10% non-nationals. Some claim it is perhaps closer to 15%. Among the fastest growing religious communities in Ireland between 2002 and 2006 were the Apostolic or Pentecostal Churches, with a growth rate of 157%. The other rates of changes were also significant: Orthodox, 99%; Hindu, 96%; Atheist, 85%; Lutheran, 72%; Muslim, 69%.

Immigrants have contributed to religious revival in Ireland, bringing enrichment to Christian denominations. A new development in inter-Church relations regarding immigrants has been a three-year, parish-based integration project, established in the Republic by a committee of the Irish Inter-Church Meeting. It is drawing attention to new models of intercultural integration developing at local parish level across the Churches.

Dietrich Bonhoeffer often spoke of *Christus präsens* in the community. Jesus died for our sins, but now 'Christ exists as Community'. The space we inhabit in the experience of God, that we have through faith in Jesus Christ, is a realm filled with the Spirit that Christ poured out through his death and resurrection. We enter the event of Jesus Christ with 'his commandment,' as John tells us: 'that we believe in the name of his Son Jesus Christ and that we love one another, just as he told us to' (1 Jn 3:23). It is by this 'love that you have for one another, everyone will know that you are my disciples' (Jn 13:34-35). The more the culture of mutual love grows between Christians, the more there will be a qualitative leap in the visibility of the Risen Christ in each of our communities with new outreach in fraternity, friendship and sense of purpose. This is not only true among individual Christians, but applies also among Churches. The more we love one another as Churches, loving each other's Church as our own, the more the gospel will impact around us because, again, as John tells us, mutual love enables God's love to be 'complete in us' (1 Jn 4:12).

Bishop Tony Farquhar

Bishop Tony Farquhar has been a significant player in inter-Church relations, particularly in the past twenty-five years. Born in Belfast in 1940, his early surroundings (including the sporting background of his late father), studies and pastoral experience brought him into contact at many levels with members of other Churches at an early stage of his life and fashioned his interest in things ecumenical. His studies for priesthood first in Belfast and then in Rome were at a time when the Catholic Church was entering into the Ecumenical Movement.

After his ordination in 1965, his appointments in parish work, an industrial training school, hospital chaplaincy, teaching for five years in student chaplaincy in Queen's University, Belfast and eight years as chaplain/lecturer in religious education in the then New University of Ulster, Coleraine, all brought him into lively interaction with brothers and sisters of other Churches. Not least in this regard was his cross-community curricular work for schools.

Particular mention must be made of his friendship with Rev. Ray Davey, founder of the Corrymeela Community. On the occasion of the ceremony of his ordination as Auxiliary Bishop in Down and Connor in May 1983, Bishop Tony pointed out that it was in his company that he had come to 'an ever-increasing realisation that respect for another's tradition is in no way dependent upon betrayal of one's own'.

It was most appropriate, therefore, that shortly after his Episcopal ordination, Bishop Tony was appointed first, member and soon after, chairman of the Commission on Ecumenism of the Irish Episcopal Conference, and likewise of its Advisory Committee on Ecumenism. He soon became a member of the Irish Inter-Church (formerly Ballymascanlon) Committee and Co-Chairman of its Standing Committee on Mixed Marriages. Over the past ten years, he has served both as Catholic Co-Chairman of the Roman Catholic Church's Dialogue with World Alliance of Reformed Churches and a member of the International Anglican Roman Catholic Commission for Unity and Mission. He served for many years as one of the two Irish Catholic Observers at the Council of Churches for Britain and Ireland and has represented Ireland at three of the European CCEE/CEC (Council of European Bishops' Conferences/Conference of European Churches) Ecumenical Encounters.

A Realist

When it comes to inter-Church relations, Bishop Tony is a realist. He knows that the legacy of centuries of division, suspicion and mistrust will not disappear overnight. He believes that, in many cases, the starting point of ecumenical work is something akin to 'pre-evangelising'. He labels it 'pre-ecumenising' – the attempt to articulate the laborious task of enabling people to find some sort of common social ground across religious traditions, enabling them to remove the 'bogeyman' image of 'the other' and find the trust that will make further and deeper dialogue possible.

The kind of pre-ecumenising that Bishop Tony has in mind extends to a wide range of activities: music, drama, dance, language, culture. Quite often, a shared common interest can bring people together in a comfortable manner that later opens into deeper exchange. And, of course, there's sport. Bishop Tony is a well known Dundee United fan and has certainly forged ecumenical links through his passion for sport and his favourite team.

He tells the story of an occasion a few years ago at Casement Park at an Antrim versus Derry Ulster Football Championship replay. He was seated directly behind President McAleese and her husband. A few minutes before the teams took to the field, a local official came down and whispered something to the President. 'Oh the Lord be good to him', she exclaimed quietly. He then turned to Bishop Tony and told him that the ace motorcycling road racer from Armoy, Joey Dunlop, had been killed in a race accident in Europe and that there would be a minute's silence before the match. It would be difficult to think of two points further apart on the sporting map of Ulster than thousands of Antrim and Derry GAA fans and a road-racing cyclist from Armoy, but the silence was impeccably observed (the memory is even more poignant in the light of the sudden death of Joey's brother, Robert, in similar circumstances). For Bishop Tony, moments of trust and respect such as that are pre-ecumenising moments that give us hope that anything is possible.

However, ecumenism is not just about pre-ecumenising; it is also about speaking and respectfully proclaiming your conviction. For over twenty years he has been a Catholic religious adviser at

Ulster Television, where over the years he has been accompanied by Bishops Ken Good and James Mahaffy and Rev. Drs Edmund Mawhinney and John Dunlop. He believes that some of the most forthright, direct and challenging ecumenical discussions in which he has been involved have taken place over lunch, following upon some of the Religious Advisory Panel meetings at Ulster Television. It is important to offer out of respect and in honesty in dialogue what you consider deepest in your life. Bishop Tony also found great inspiration in the example of close co-operation of the Catholic Archbishop Worlock and the Anglican Bishop Sheppard in Liverpool, along with the prominent Methodist minister, Dr John Newton.

Working on Building up Inter-Church Relations

There are many ways to build up inter-Church relations. Bishop Tony has been quite involved in the Ulster Project Conference, an ecumenical venture where school children from Belfast spend some time over the summer with American families. He was also a member of the United States-Northern Ireland Presbyterian/Roman Catholic committee, which worked on a common project enabling students from Irish universities to travel to the United States for a year.

It has been important to Bishop Tony to encourage local clergy fraternals for all they have contributed in common study, discussion and prayer. He sees the value of building up these contacts between Church ministers. He often witnessed at first hand how, on occasions such as funerals of assassination victims, members of clergy fraternals would go together to give support by their presence and prayers, and this was much appreciated by bereaved families. These fraternals have opened and enlarged themselves in recent years to embrace both lay and clerical membership and they have been particularly effective.

Interestingly, in the pastoral ecumenical context, Bishop Tony has noted that it is often in extra-parochial ministries that ecumenism is strongest. Close to his heart is the Fleming Fulton School, a school for children with physical disabilities that sees good ecumenical involvement. In terms of furthering good inter-Church relations, he values the place of religious communities, student chaplaincy, hospital chaplaincy and, perhaps the most unusual one of all in the North, prison chaplaincy – particularly when one bears in mind the very circumstances that have led many of the prisoners to have found their way into that situation in the first place.

There is a priority in all of this. While the importance of intellect and social action should not be underestimated, it is nevertheless always necessary to balance these with spirituality. This was at the heart of Vatican II's proposal for ecumenism, as laid out in *Unitatis Redintegratio*.

In that sense, Bishop Tony knows that the struggle for Christian unity is not quite the same as work to improve community relations.[14] Certainly, ecumenical advances can contribute to an amelioration of civil difficulties, but he has always underlined that the primary task of ecumenists is to try to follow Christ's prayer, 'May they all be one' and not try to use ecumenism as a means to fulfil another end. An increasing current risk is that, after thirty years or so – years when strife and violence were labelled as a Catholic versus Protestant struggle – being Catholic now can be seen as being divisive in a society where everything must be seen to be inclusive and integrated. Building a shared future, however, will always recognise the distinctive contribution of each Church.

Ecumenical 'Dos' and 'Don'ts'

On the basis of Vatican II, Bishop Tony lives by a set of 'dos' and 'don'ts' in ecumenism. Among the 'dos' he includes: dialogue; collaboration for the common good; prayer (in private and communally); work for reform and renewal; patience; prudence; taking the first steps; focus on inward conversion; openness to being edified by others; living charity; humility and getting to know others. Among the 'don'ts' he mentions: expressing the other's viewpoint wrongly; carelessness in how you speak of others; imprudent excess of zeal; placing obstacles and prejudices in the way of the future.

Earlier this year, he wrote up his 'ecum-mandments' in the form of Decalogue, which runs as follows:[15]

1. You shall not confuse ecumenism with community, political or social relations;
2. You shall have a healthy pride in and respect for your own tradition;
3. You shall have pride in and respect for other traditions as for your own;
4. You shall not be smug or self-righteous within your own tradition;
5. You shall not be smug or self-righteous in your relations with other traditions;
6. You shall not claim to represent anyone other than yourself when you have moved outside the official teaching of your own Church;
7. You shall pray for unity in prayer within your own tradition;
8. You shall pray for unity in prayer between your traditions;
9. You shall be thankful for what has already been achieved ecumenically;
10. You shall smile ecumenically and some day the people of God will smile with you.

Joy

Anyone who has met Bishop Tony knows that joy is a feature of his life and ministry. He genuinely believes that one of the greatest ecumenical contributions is to be cheerful in each other's company when we come together. He has never accepted that angst-ridden features are amongst the marks of a good ecumenist. Indeed, he would make his own Teresa of Avila's prayer to be delivered from 'santos encapitados' – gloomy saints dressed in shrouds. Joy is the great gift of the Spirit and it is vital to ecumenism. As Bishop Tony puts it in the last of the 'ecum-mandments' listed above: 'You shall smile ecumenically and some day the People of God will smile with you'.

Every occasion presents the opportunity to see the humorous side. For instance, Bishop Tony tells the story of one occasion in his university chaplaincy days when a highly intelligent student, on discovering that the Catholic chaplain had golfed the previous day with the Presbyterian chaplain, asked, 'Would you actually spend your day off with him?' 'Of course', came the reply. 'That's brilliant', the student replied, amazed. Bishop Tony comments wryly and, in his self-effacing way, that was probably one of his more significant moments of ecumenical leadership through the years.

The Contents of this Book

This book has come to life as a tribute to honour Bishop Tony. The contributors eagerly responded to the invitation to contribute. There are many others who could have contributed but the inevitable limitations of trying to keep the length of the book within manageable proportions and balance prevented the net of invitations being cast too wide! Gratitude, therefore, to those who gave generously of time and idea in their contribution. Apologies to anyone who would have liked to be part of this project but was unintentionally excluded. Thanks are also due to Frances Doran of the Down and Connor Diocesan Curia, Bishop Anthony Farquhar's sister, Anne Farquhar, Catherine Gough and all at Veritas Publications.

The book attempts to open windows to some aspects of contemporary inter-Church relations. It looks at significant recent developments in international dialogue and networking among Churches. It provides updates on current developments on the ecclesial landscape of Ireland. Reflections are offered on a number of points, not least concerning the new directions opening up in Northern Ireland and those emerging in the changing scene in the Republic. No doubt there are many other themes that could also have been addressed, but the array of topics treated is already quite extensive and provides a taste of what is happening in the ecumenical world. It is hoped that, in some modest way, this work will further stimulate continuing engagement with the great cause of inter-Church relations in the light of Jesus' last will and testament: 'May they all be one' (Jn 17:21).

Notes

1. Pope John Paul II, *Crossing the Threshold of Hope* (London: Jonathan Cape, 1994), p. 153.
2. See Cardinal Kasper's Presidential Opening Speech to the Vatican II Fortieth Anniversary Conference on *Unitatis Redintegratio*,

November 2004, printed in English edition of *L'Osservatore Romano* (1 December 2004), p. 8.

3. See his first message to the members of the College of Cardinals in the Sistine Chapel the day after his election as Pope, 20 April, 2005. *Acta Apostolica Sedis* XCVII (2005), pp. 694–699, at p. 697.

4. See Vatican II's Dogmatic Constitution on Divine Revelation, *Dei Verbum*, n. 8.

5. See Vatican II's Decree on Ecumenism, *Unitatis Redintegratio*, n. 4.

6. Pope John Paul's Encyclical Letter on Commitment to Ecumenism, *Ut Unum Sint*, p. 82.

7. See Rusch, William G. (ed.), *Justification and the Future of the Ecumenical Movement : the Joint Declaration on the Doctrine of Justification* (Collegeville, Minn: Liturgical Press, 2003).

8. See text and commentaries in Donald Bolen and Gregory Cameron (eds), *Mary: Grace and Hope in Christ* (London: Continuum, 2006).

9. See his article 'Christianity – A Credible Presence?' in Dermot A. Lane (ed.), *New Century, New Society: Christian Perspectives* (Dublin: Columba Press, 1999), pp. 11–17, at p. 12.

10. See Keenan, Dan, 'President praises "remarkable new days of transition" in Northern Ireland', *Irish Times*, 30 November, 2007.

11. Appleby, R. Scott, *The Ambivalence of the Sacred: Religion, Violence, and Reconciliation* (Lanham, MD: Rowman and Littlefield, 2000), p. 16.

12. See Lederach, John Paul, *The Moral Imagination: The Art and Soul of Building Peace* (New York: Oxford University Press, 2005).

13. Vatican II's Pastoral Constitution on the Church in the Modern World, *Gaudium et Spes*, n. 78.

14. See Maria Power's work on this theme, *From Ecumenism to Community Relations: Inter-Church Relationships in Northern Ireland 1980–2005* (Dublin: Irish Academic Press, 2007).

15. See Anthony Farquhar, 'Ecum-mandments Revisited', *The Furrow*, Vol. 59 (2008), pp. 3–11.

1 Bishop Anthony Farquhar and the International Reformed-Catholic Dialogue

Cardinal Walter Kasper

I t is a pleasure to contribute a letter to the festschrift honouring Bishop Anthony Farquhar on the occasion of this significant anniversary. A notable part of his ministry as a bishop has been dedicated to ecumenical relations, not only in Ireland, but also in a larger international context. In that respect, he has cooperated with the Pontifical Council for Promoting Christian Unity in many events and studies related to the search for the unity of Christ's disciples.

One area that I wish to mention on this occasion is the third phase of International Reformed–Catholic Dialogue (1998-2006) and his willingness to serve, at the request of the PCPCU, as its Catholic Co-Chair. That dialogue produced a report, recently published, entitled 'The Church as the Community of Common Witness to the Kingdom of God'. The report is significant in several ways; I would like to point to just two.

Firstly, it makes a further contribution to an important development resulting from the previous, second phase of Reformed-Catholic dialogue, as can be seen in 'Towards a Common Understanding of the Church' (1990). The latter claimed an important convergence of two ways of understanding the Church: as *Creatura Verbi*, preferred by the Reformed, and as Sacrament of Grace, more typical of our Catholic understanding. These are not contradictory, the report claimed, but give different insights into a fuller understanding of the Church. The recent report of the third phase of dialogue goes more deeply into this matter, showing, in light of a reflection on the biblical notion of the Kingdom of God and an exploration of patristic sources, that the insights of both of these visions of the Church are important for a proper understanding of the Church. The third phase of dialogue, then, helps to show that Reformed and Catholics share important aspects of a common understanding of the Church.

A second notable feature of 'The Church as the Community of Common Witness to the Kingdom of God' is that, through exploring ways in which Reformed and Catholics have given common witness to the Kingdom of God, it presents three narratives or case studies in which this has been done in areas where conflict has taken place: South Africa, Canada and Northern Ireland. The dialogue commission held sessions in each of these settings. Bishop Farquhar was especially helpful in bringing the Commission into contact with the realities of Northern Ireland, where he has spent long years of pastoral ministry serving the people affected by the conflict. The narrative shows the evolution of ecumenical relations between the different Christian communities in Northern Ireland in efforts to witness to the Gospel in the midst of the tragedies. Difficulties for ecumenical relations still exist, but more common witness is given now because of the impact of the ecumenical movement. A new spirit of cooperation and understanding has made headway among the various communities due to the commitment of many dedicated men and women, not the least of whom is Bishop Farquhar.

In giving these examples, I wish to thank Bishop Farquhar again, in the name of the Pontifical Council for Promoting Christian Unity, for serving as Co-Chair of the dialogue and guiding it to a successful conclusion.

Congratulations on twenty-five fruitful years of episcopal ministry. May there be many more.

2   *A Personal Testimony*

Rev. Ray Davey

A very important relationship for me has been with Bishop Tony Farquhar, whom I first met when he was one of the Catholic chaplains at Queen's University. I have learnt much from him: what his faith means to him, his dedication and spirituality, his deep love and concern for young people, his zest for life, be it folk music or football, his lovely sense of humour and the sincerity of his friendship. I have seen the price he pays for his vocation and the strength of his discipline, and I cannot forget the way in which he accepted me as a friend and a brother in Christ.

This acceptance did not mean that he expected me to give up my convictions. Nor did I think he should surrender his. We accepted each other with our differences. I still have many problems with his tradition and he with mine. Even so, we can accept each other as followers of the one Lord and face our differences in the spirit of trust and openness. Hence the importance of real meeting – this means risk-taking, finding common ground and being willing to share our lives, our interests, our concerns and our faith. In this way, we learn to grow together.

The good Lord gives each of us those little hints from time to time; signs that He is about, if we have the eyes to see them. This is such a one that was given to my wife Kathleen and I, along with Tony Farquhar, who was at that time one of the Catholic chaplains at Queen's University. The three of us had travelled to Lausanne in Switzerland to tell about the work of Corrymeela. It was the Week of Prayer for Christian Unity and we had a very full programme of meetings, services and interviews.

One afternoon we had a pause in our itinerary and our gracious hosts decided that we needed a break, so they drove us away, up into the snow-capped mountains and through a quiet peaceful landscape, until we came to a little village called Romainmôtier. When we got out of the car, they led us to a beautiful Romanesque church which they thought would interest us. No sooner had we entered the foyer than we began to understand why they had brought us to this place. On the wall immediately facing us as we entered was a large map of ancient Europe. Ireland, on the edge of it, was marked out with a red circle.

Across the Netherlands, Belgium, France, Germany and Switzerland certain places were underlined. As we studied it we could see that it was the story of the Irish missionaries of the Celtic period in the fifth to ninth centuries, who had journeyed from their different houses in Ireland. We can think of Columbanus who came from the monastery in Bangor, Co Down, and had established Christian Communities in many parts of Europe.

One of his followers, St Gall, made a profound and lasting impression in Switzerland. You may guess how moved we were to learn that this Christian House in Romainmôtier had been founded by Irish missionaries. Back then Ireland was described as 'the land of saints and scholars' and the Irish known as the great missionary race.

In the silence we thought about it and, above all, the sadness of our visit. Here we were many centuries later, representing the Catholic and Protestant traditions in Ireland, coming to this country to try to explain the division and tragedy of our land, the same Ireland, centuries later. Before we left the church, we stood together with joined hands in the Sanctuary, and after saying the Lord's Prayer we prayed that through the healing of the Spirit our land might again become 'the land of saints and scholars'.

3 *Living the Ecumenical Dream*
Bishop Gerard Clifford

I first came to meet Tony Farquhar when I was involved in organising a series of ecumenical talks between the Archdiocese of Armagh and St Anne's Church of Ireland Cathedral in Belfast. In the late 1970s, Canon William Arlow and myself had been asked to set up a conversation between St Patrick's Cathedral in Armagh and St Anne's Church of Ireland Cathedral in Belfast in an effort to bring people together from the different traditions to discuss issues of an ecumenical, theological and social nature. One of the series of talks was under the title 'The Way Forward – working together for peace and reconciliation in Northern Ireland'. Tony was sharing the platform with the Rev. Ray Davey, founder of the Corrymeela Community in Ballycastle. In his lecture, Tony said that we should always be clear that ecumenical work is first and foremost a response to the gospel imperative 'that all may be one' (Jn 17:21) and we should not confuse ecumenism with community, political or social relations. That was in 1983. It was a theme that he would pursue on many occasions in the years to follow.

In May 1983, Tony Farquhar was appointed Auxiliary Bishop in Down and Connor. Within days of his ordination as Bishop, Cardinal O Fiaich's brother died suddenly and Tony was asked to take up some Confirmation ceremonies in the Archdiocese. It marked the beginning of a happy and lasting relationship between Tony Farquhar and the Archdiocese of Armagh.

The Irish Bishops' Conference

When a new bishop joins the Irish Bishops' Conference he is appointed to one of the Commissions or agencies that make up the working groups of the Conference. Because of Tony's previous involvement in ecumenism, it was taken for granted that he would be appointed to ecumenism, and so he was. He was appointed to the Advisory Committee on Ecumenism and shortly afterwards to the Irish Inter-Church Meeting (the official contact between the Catholic Church and the member Churches of the Irish Council of Churches). Today the Inter-Church Meeting is the main force behind the work of the Churches for ecumenism at national level. It meets three times yearly in Dundalk and helps to address theological, biblical and social issues impinging on the lives of Christians in Ireland.

At national level, one of the other important points of contact between the Churches is the Inter-Church Standing Committee on Mixed Marriage. The Committee was set up in 1975 to help address trends in inter-Church marriages that were giving rise to concern between the Churches. The Committee continues to meet to this day and is a valuable point of contact in helping to address neuralgic issues in this area. Tony was appointed to the Committee and twenty-five years later is still a member.

Over the years, ecumenism has been the focus of his work within the Bishops' Conference. At the regular meetings of the bishops in Maynooth, Tony scrutinises every topic with the incisive eye of a master consultant to see if they have any ecumenical implications. Topics of a most non-descript nature are subjected to rigorous examination. In some ways Tony reminds me of the famous verse in the Old Irish poem *Pangur Ban*, from one of the glosses in a manuscript in the library in St Paul's Monastery in the former Carinthia (presently Austria), dating back to the beginning of the ninth century. The scribe compares himself to his beloved cat, Pangur Ban. He says:

Me and Pangur Ban my cat
'Tis a like task we are at:
Hunting mice is his delight,
Hunting words I sit all night.

Like the old Irish monk, Tony never misses a word or an opportunity to apply his expertise.

Involvement with the CTBI

One of the implications of involvement in ecumenism over the years has been the opportunity to travel abroad for various ecumenical initiatives. One of the most engaging opportunities was the setting up of an ecumenical initiative for Great Britain and Ireland.

Back in the 1980s an inter-Church process was established under the title 'Not Strangers but Pilgrims'. In 1990, the British Council of Churches went out of existence and was replaced by the Council of Churches for Britain and Ireland, in which the Catholic Church in England, Wales and Scotland were full members. Over those years there was a prolonged debate on how Ireland might be involved. There were extended discussions at the Irish Bishops' Conference to see how Ireland might contribute to this work. In Ireland, the Church of Ireland and the Methodist Church became full members of the new initiative. The Presbyterian Church and the Religious Society of Friends declined to join.

In all the debate, the Irish Bishops' Conference was emphatic that the Irish Inter-Church Meeting at home had served the Churches well over the years and was better geared to answer the current needs in Ireland. The Bishops were also of the opinion that it would not wish to jeopardise their involvement with all the Churches in Ireland. Eventually the Catholic Bishops decided to become Associate Members of the Council of Churches for Britain and Ireland. In more recent times, the Council of Churches for Britain and Ireland was restructured. It is now known as Churches Together in Britain and Ireland. The Catholic Church continues to be an associate member.

Making History in Germany

As a member of the Inter-Church Meeting, Tony was also involved in regular meetings in continental Europe, particularly in Germany. On a biannual basis, ecumenical gatherings are held throughout Germany, alternatively organised by the Catholic Church (*Katholikentag*) and by the Protestant Churches *(Kirchentag).* These are massive gatherings spread over several days to celebrate and explore one's Christian commitment and explore the challenges faced by Churches together. Guest speakers are invited to lead the discussion.

On one occasion, after the official Conference had drawn to a close, Cardinal O'Fiaich had been invited to preach at the Vigil Mass in Munchengladbach. Bishop Tony had discovered that Munchengladbach were playing Eintracht at home on that Sunday afternoon and he couldn't resist the temptation to attend the match. He had hoped to be back in time for the end of the ceremony. Having been detained by the welcoming courtesy and hospitality of home team officials and directors, he arrived in the middle of the ceremony. Cardinal O'Fiaich spotted him in the distance and halted for a moment. Having first pointed out that there might be some young people present at the Mass who would be more interested in what had happened at the Stadium than in the history of Irish monasticism in that part of Germany, he asked Bishop Tony to announce the score. Sheepishly, Tony emerged from behind a pillar and announced a one-all draw. There was a moment's silence and then tumultuous applause as the gathering realised their team had won on aggregate.

It was a moment in Church history in Germany that will be long remembered. Until then results of matches were never part of the ecumenical scene and certainly were never announced publicly in a Church gathering. Once more the Irish were making history.

With the Bishops' Conference of England and Wales

Bishop Tony is well known as a preacher at ecumenical services and at diocesan retreats in Ireland and England. In 2006 he was invited by the Bishops' Conference in England and Wales to give a pastoral reflection on various challenges facing the Church in the third millennium. I was there as a representative of the Irish Bishops' Conference. The gathering of all the bishops lasted five days and was held in the English College in Valladolid.

Topics included were the experience of a diocesan bishop in a secularised society of Western Europe and the challenge of witnessing to the faith in a materialistic world. After every lecture Tony was to give a spiritual interpretation of the talk. He related the various presentations to various encyclicals, decrees and Apostolic Letters of Pope John Paul II and predictably teased out the ecumenical implications. It was an impressive performance, a veritable *tour de force*.

Memorable Trips

For some years Tony and myself have travelled together to various ecumenical gatherings in Europe. One of the most memorable was a visit to the then Soviet Union in 1989 when, as part of a delegation from the Churches, we were invited by the Russian Orthodox Church to see first hand the relationship between the Orthodox and Christian Churches in various parts of the Union. We visited several museums, had a grand tour of different Orthodox institutions and then divided into groups to visit outside the Moscow area. Tony and myself were part of the delegation that went to Latvia and Riga.

We visited the local Catholic Seminary and saw the spartan facilities. They had few books and few comforts. We brought along some liturgical books and vestments given to us by the Armagh Apostolic Work Society. All the gifts were greatly appreciated by the priests and students. Over the years some of us used to complain about our own basic facilities while in Seminary in the 1960s. After the experience of the Soviet Union we came to regard ourselves as very lucky indeed.

Another memorable outing in recent times was a visit to Sibiu in Romania for the Third Ecumenical Assembly (4–9 September, 2007). Thirty-seven representatives from the Inter-Church meeting gathered for a conference on 'The Light of Christ shines upon all'. Over the five days there were various reflections on the theme, and in smaller discussion groups called 'fora' there was an opportunity to pursue one's particular interest.

A special forum was dedicated to reconciliation in other parts of the world and Tony was one of the delegates to make a presentation on reconciliation in Northern Ireland. In the ensuing discussion, it was obvious that Northern Ireland could well be a paradigm that might pave the way forward towards peace and reconciliation in other parts of the world.

Sibiu was a good experience, even if at times it struggled to cope with the large delegation of two thousand five hundred people involved. The experience got off to a shaky start with the bus journey from Bucharest to Sibiu in Transylvania. We were told the journey would be some hours. After five hours somebody asked the driver how far we had to go. He said maybe another hour or so. It was another two hours before we eventually got to our base and were allocated a pleasant *auberge* outside the city.

One of the abiding memories of our visit was on the Saturday when we were invited by the Greek Catholic Church to join them for the liturgy in honour of the Birthday of Mary, the Mother of God. The splendour of the liturgy was awesome. The attention to liturgical detail was impressive. The harmonious chants enthralled us all. The Mass combined the beautiful ceremonial of the Greek tradition with the solemn liturgy that we often associate with the pre-Vatican II period. It was the combination of the best parts from the eastern and western traditions. It was a memorable occasion.

Conclusion

There are many other memories of Tony's involvement in ecumenism over the years. On many of those occasions I had the pleasure of being involved. All of them were full of fun, at times hilarious and at times very serious. All of them bear witness to Tony's own commitment to respond to the call of Christ 'that all may be one'. I have every confidence that Tony will continue to challenge all of us as we travel on our own journey of faith.

DEVELOPMENTS

4   Renewing the Church through Dialogue

Archbishop Mario Conti

W hen I was ordained at the Church of San Marcello on the Via del Corso in Rome in the autumn of 1958, it was during a period of *sede vacante* in the Papacy. Pius XII had just died and John XXIII had yet to be elected. My priesthood, one might say, was born on a cusp.

None of us who were ordained that October day could have imagined the roller-coaster ride we were about to experience, propelled by the Holy Spirit and under the steering hand of Angelo Roncalli, who confounded the pundits who had cast him in the role of caretaker Pope by becoming one of the great reforming Pontiffs of the twentieth century. Few paragraphs express more vividly the atmosphere of hope, which permeated the Church in those days, than Pope Paul's dramatic but moving closing address of the Council:

> Just as the sound of the bell goes out through the skies, reaching each one within the radius of its sound waves, so at this moment does our greeting go out to each and every one of you. To those who receive it and to those who do not, it resounds pleadingly in the ear of every man. From this Catholic centre of Rome, no one, in principle, is unreachable; in principle, all can and must be reached. For the Catholic Church, no one is a stranger, no one is excluded, no one is far away.[1]

There are few areas in which the dramatic change in the Church's life occasioned by the reforms of Vatican II have been more keenly felt than in the area of ecumenism. Those words of Pope Paul, 'No one is a stranger, no one is excluded, no one is far away,' were to become prophetic guides in my own life and that of Bishop Farquhar over the next forty years, as we ploughed the ecumenical furrow together, separated only by those few miles of sea between Cairnryan and Larne.

We both grew up in cultures where religious differences were highly significant, though there could be no comparing the north-east of Scotland with Northern Ireland, where such differences could lead to community apartheid and even violent conflict. Nonetheless, at the level of religious expression, our experiences would have been very similar.

I recall as a boy we could not even say the *Our Father* together. When I was taken by my music master to his Kirk to entertain the Ladies' Guild with my efforts on the violin, I was gently ushered into the darkness without, while the assembled company recited the *Our Father*. To this day I am not sure whether this was on the instruction of my concerned mother or out of the respectful concern of the ladies, lest my little 'papist' ears were offended. I suspect the former, since we were very careful in those days not to share in worship.

In my appointment as a parish priest I certainly did experience in the very north of Scotland what had not been my experience as a child, and there was more than one occasion in which I had to enter, with somewhat reluctant but supportive parishioners, into town halls in order to defend the faith against those renegades who had been invited to come to tell of the wickedness of the Catholic Church!

On one such occasion I was invited by my neighbouring Presbyterian minister to join him and the speaker afterwards for a cup of tea. I suspect the latter was more embarrassed than I was since he never returned. On the other hand, the minister and I became respectful friends.

Vatican II

But the scene was already changing. My appointment as Parish Priest came in the very autumn that saw in Rome the opening of the

Second Vatican Council, and two years later, on 21 November 1964, the Vatican Council solemnly promulgated the Decree on Ecumenism, *Unitatis Redintegratio*. It was one of the most far reaching in effect of the Council documents. The document boldly states in its introduction that 'Christ the Lord founded one Church and one Church only', and that division contradicts the will of the Lord, 'scandalizes the world and damages that most holy cause, the preaching of the Gospel ... The restoration of unity among all Christians is one of the principal concerns of the Second Vatican Council' (n. 1).

The Council provided the roadmap for the Church's journey in the twenty-first century.[2] On several occasions, Pope John Paul said that our ecumenical venture is irrevocable,[3] and that ecumenism was 'one of the pastoral priorities' of his Pontificate.[4] The current Holy Father, Benedict XVI, also committed himself to the work of unity in his inaugural homily as Pope: 'Let us rejoice because of your promise, which does not disappoint, and let us do all we can to pursue the path towards the unity you have promised'.

I remember being forcibly struck by Pope John Paul II's statement of the 'irrevocable commitment' of the Catholic Church to the ecumenical journey, as I had the privilege of reading aloud his message to the Eighth Assembly of the World Council of Churches in Harare in 1998. I vividly recall the response that literally thousands of delegates gave to a message that called upon them to work without rest, and to grow deeper in union with one another and with the Lord, who prayed for the unity of his followers on the night he was betrayed.

As Catholics we have had to ask ourselves some probing questions as we have made this pilgrimage of faith together with our separated brethren. We have sensed the need to establish the Catholic principles of ecumenism as formulated in the Decree *Unitatis Redintegratio* for the guidance of our people.

It is appropriate from this vantage point – more than forty years after the promulgation of the document – to look back on the ecumenical journey which the Church has taken, and ask: 'Ecumenism, *unde venisti et quo vadis?*'(From where have you come and where are you going?).

And it is helpful to recall the historical developments which led to the decree's promulgation back in the winter of 1964, for clearly it did not appear out of thin air.

It fits into the context of the ecumenical movement that came into being in the twentieth century outside the Catholic Church, a movement which many would say was born in Edinburgh at the Missionary Conference in 1910, and which reached a decisive coming-of-age with the creation of the World Council of Churches in 1948.

This movement was long regarded with suspicion by the Catholic Church. But its acceptance by the Second Vatican Council is rooted in the Catholic theology of the nineteenth century. In particular, Johann Adam Möhler and John Henry Newman should be cited as significant influences.

But it would be wrong to see the Catholic Church as playing purely a catch-up role. Even before the Second Vatican Council, the Popes encouraged prayers for unity in addition to the 'Week of Prayer for Christian Unity'. Leo XIII and Benedict XV paved the way for ecumenical openness. Pius XI explicitly approved the 'Malines Conversations' (1921–1926) with the Anglicans.

Pius XII went a step further. In an Instruction of 1950, he expressly supported the ecumenical movement, emphasising that it originated in the action of the Holy Spirit.

As Cardinal Walter Kasper put it recently, while reflecting on forty years of ecumenism since Vatican II, 'It would be erroneous to overlook this fundamental continuity and see the Council as a radical break with tradition and identifying it with the advent of a new Church'.[5] Yet something new did begin with the Council: not a *new* Church but a *renewed* Church.

As we read in *Dei Verbum*, the Vatican Council's Dogmatic Constitution on Divine Revelation: 'As the centuries go by, the Church is always advancing towards the plenitude of divine truth, until eventually the words of God are fulfilled in her' (n. 8).

Lumen Gentium, the Constitution on the nature of the Church, sees the community of faith as a 'germinating seed' and a 'pilgrim', a harbinger of the fulfilled promise, and calls for the Church to be inserted more deeply within the drama of history, not aloof from it.

That means that the Church must speak to the age, and it must learn the vocabulary of ecumenical dialogue. This would be very much part of Pope John's *aggiornamento*.

One of the most significant insights of the Council Fathers in *Unitatis Redintegratio* was to recognise in other Churches and ecclesial communions those elements essential to the Church which Christ founded and which form part of her treasured patrimony. This has allowed us to recognise one another as radically belonging to the same divided family – so that we can speak of 'separated brethren'.

As Cardinal Kasper puts it:

> In ecumenism, the Church enters into an exchange of gifts with the Separated Churches (*UUS*, 28, 57), enriches them, but also reciprocally makes their gifts its own, adds them to its Catholic fullness and thus fully realises its own catholicity (*UR*, 4).[6]

To do so means to recognise that other Christians are not rivals, but fellow pilgrims called, like us, to unity in the body of Christ.

Prizing Unity
The Catholic Church has always prized the unity of the Church and prayed for it according to the mind of her divine master. Seeing herself, rightly, as already possessing such unity to a remarkable degree – a communion of faith, of hope and of charity, spreading geographically worldwide and extending into the future like a great river which had its source in the very wellsprings of the faith, namely the apostles themselves.

Vatican II denied none of this, but sought a way to recognise and embrace in others the gifts, which the Catholic Church had already received and of which the Church, to a measure, has been in every instance the conduit.

Of great significance is the conciliar statement that the Church of Christ 'subsists in' and not simply 'is' the Catholic Church. There has been much reflection and discussion of this phrase which seeks to accommodate two truths: one, that the Church of Jesus Christ has its concrete location in the Catholic Church, in that

Communion of Churches which profess the Apostolic faith and over which the successor of St Peter presides. And two, that already by our common baptism and the gift of the Spirit we are, with our separated brethren, in a real but imperfect communion.

The ecumenical path we travel is not without risks however. From a faith perspective, the dangers are essentially twofold. The first danger consists in treating those elements of our 'treasured patrimony' as being simply heirlooms, which, however valuable, can be set aside, or placed in a museum. Some elements of our faith simply cannot be set aside: issues such as the Apostolic Tradition of faith and practice; the Church's hierarchical structure (episcopacy and the Petrine Ministry); the sacraments; the Mass as sacrifice as well as communion; sanctifying grace; the communion of saints; devotion to Our Lady and so on.

When we use the word 'tradition', we are not talking of what the Italians might call the *beni culturali* and we the 'heritage' of the Church. Rather we mean the dynamic handing on of the faith from one generation to the next. St Vincent of Lerins, in speaking of the development of that tradition, likened it to the way in which a human person grows from infancy, through childhood, into adulthood and then mature years. The development is from within, it is dynamic, coherent, organic; it is not the result of accretions and additions, nor indeed of subtractions! It is a reality in which the Church already possesses what she is destined to be in her perfection.

In contrast to the first danger, namely that of looking back and treating tradition as something from the past, the second danger is to consider Church unity as something only realisable at the end of time. The truth is that the Church lives in the present. She inhabits this world. While she is an eschatological reality, she already possesses the catholicity, apostolicity, unity and sanctity which we profess of her in the creed, albeit imperfectly. In like manner, each member of the Church is forever being called to perfection.

For example, the Catholic Church, already one, would have her unity enhanced in the coming together of all who profess their faith in Christ and are baptised, and in like manner with regard to the other marks of the Church – namely her catholicity, her sanctity and apostolicity.

Cardinal Kasper puts it succinctly when he says:

> The Catholic principles of ecumenism, as formulated by the Council and later by Pope John Paul II, are therefore clear and unequivocal in their rejection of irenicism and relativism, which reduce everything to banality. The ecumenical movement does not throw overboard anything which has been valued and cherished by the Church in its previous history, it remains faithful to the truth that has been acknowledged in history ... The ecumenical movement and its avowed goal, the unity of the disciples of Jesus Christ, remain inscribed within the furrow of tradition.[7]

To recognise tradition in this dynamic sense places a corrective on any superficial attempt to use a sort of checklist with regard to the elements belonging to the Catholic Church which might be identified elsewhere, for example, in other churches and ecclesial communities. We ought rather to see what we recognise as our own, shared manifestations of the Holy Spirit – the very profession of faith in Christ as the Son of God is not possible unless, as Jesus taught, it is revealed to us by the Father. No one can say 'Jesus is Lord', says the apostle, unless he is moved by the Holy Spirit.

While sharing the fruits of the Spirit, nobly recognising them in one another, the most significant recognition is our radical sharing in the gift of the Holy Spirit itself. This sharing is described by the Greek word *koinonia* (*communio* in Latin).

Communion is a word familiar to us with reference to the sacrament of the Lord's body and blood, and a desire to share it is now commonplace among Christians, but the very etymology of the word directs us to that underlying reality, namely to our being one in the gift of the Spirit: 'May they be one, as You Father are in me, and I in You', as the Lord prayed at the Last Supper.

So the unity for which Christ prayed is very far from schemes of federal association or man-made plans for sharing resources. Even campaigning for Eucharistic hospitality can lead us to miss what is really significant, and what really matters in our desire to act ecumenically. It is in grasping this that we can appreciate the

Council's insistence on conversion of heart as the necessary pre-requisite of ecumenism and of its description of prayer as the 'soul of the ecumenical movement'.

Dialogue on the Basis of our Common Baptism

Dialogue is the privileged means of ecumenical encounter. The Joint Working Group, the liaison body between the World Council of Churches (WCC) and the Catholic Church set up in the wake of the Council and of which I was for some time co-moderator, worked for six years on a document on dialogue which it presented to the Ninth Assembly of the World Council at Porto Alegre in Brazil and to the Pontifical Council for the Promotion of Christian Unity (2006).

The very word 'dialogue' suggests conversation between two or more people and being sensitive to what each person says. The document notes the progress that has been made between Churches both at local and at international levels through dialogue. There has been, for example, the Faith and Order statement, 'Baptism, Eucharist and Ministry', referred to by the ecumenical cognoscenti as 'BEM'. It is a document which has still to make its full impact on all the Churches in whose name the dialogue was carried through. In a sense we have already returned to this document by addressing anew the ecclesial significance of our common baptism.

At present a joint commission on doctrine between the Catholic Church and the Church of Scotland is studying the theme of baptism, having been prompted to do so and enriched by the document prepared by the Joint Working Group for the Ninth Assembly of the WCC. It is formally entitled 'Ecclesiological and Ecumenical Implications of a Common Baptism', and is, in my view, one of the most significant documents the Joint Working Group has produced during the time of its existence, namely since the end of Vatican II.

This document calls the Churches to return to a recognition of the nature of the sacrament, which we recognise as being validly administered across the Churches and which in our Catholic under-standing certainly carries the gift of the Holy Spirit and inserts the baptised person, whether child or adult, into the Church – the Church which we profess in the creed as 'one, holy, catholic and apostolic'.

We have to, however, face the fact that in the very administration of the sacrament, those who are baptised are also inserted into local communities of faith, and it is these local communities or local Churches that are divided, creating the anomaly of a fractured unity at the very point of insertion into the Church.

But if we take the ecclesiological implications of baptism seriously, we can anticipate fresh ecumenical impulses, certainly in the field of doctrine, which, above all, our dialogues must embrace. Both *Lumen Gentium* and *Unitatis Redintegratio* point to baptism as funda-mental to our understanding of the Church and of Christian unity:

> It is the sacrament of faith, whereby those who have been baptised belong to the one body of Christ which is the Church. Non-Catholic Christians are therefore not outside of the one Church; they already belong to it in the most fundamental way.

These words of Cardinal Kasper lead to his conclusion:

> On the basis of one common baptism, ecumenism goes far beyond simple goodwill and friendliness; it is not a form of church diplomacy; it has an ontological foundation and an ontological depth; it is an event of the Spirit.[8]

We can recognise such a document and what flows from it as being fruits of dialogue in this instance between the Catholic Church and the WCC. The Catholic Church, while itself not a full member of the World Council, is nevertheless represented with full mem-bership status in some of its agencies, most notably that of the Faith and Order Commission, which comprises a number of Catholic theologians.

Catholic membership of national and local councils of Churches has increased over the years, and the final document presented to our respective parent bodies by the Joint Working Group was entitled, 'Inspired by the same vision: a study of Roman Catholic participation in national and regional councils of churches'.

The document points out that whereas, 'at the time of the Council, the Roman Catholic Church did not take part in any national council of churches, at the present time, of approximately 120 national councils of churches, the Roman Catholic Church is a full member in 70, and the number is growing.'

Membership has not always been easy for either side, if we can talk in such terms. The reason being that our ecclesiologies can differ very greatly. Those who have an episcopal Church order reach decisions and take them by a process, which is very different from those Churches, like the Church of Scotland or the Presbyterian Church in Ireland, who resolve their outstanding administrative and even doctrinal matters through debate and decision in assembly.

However, it is the discovery on both parts of such differences between us that enables us to understand why, at times, we fail to speak with one voice or act together, despite the Lund Principle that, as far as possible, we should only do separately what cannot be done together. This seems to be a principle more observed in the breach than in the practice.

Bishop Tony Farquhar has been involved in many of these dialogues, both at national and international levels. He has been a very sensitive and warmly appreciated co-chairman of the bi-lateral commission of the Catholic Church and the World Alliance of Reformed Churches. He is also a member of IARCCUM (International Anglican Roman Catholic Commission for Unity and Mission), which has happily produced a weighty document in recent months charting the development of relations between the Catholic Church and the Churches of the Anglican Communion, and pointing to practical steps that can be taken to deepen our appreciation of one another and work towards unity, despite the difficulties that have arisen over recent decisions of some of the Churches of the Anglican Communion.

While these engagements are time consuming, and at times perhaps frustrating, they are nonetheless not only necessary but enriching both for the Churches, which we severally represent, and for our own lives. How deep are the friendships we have made, recalling to mind those words of the psalmist, 'Behold how good and how lovely it is when brothers dwell together in unity' (Ps 133:1).

Many are the ecumenical friends that Bishop Tony has made over his years as a bishop and as an active ecumenist, both in Ireland

and on the international scene; there is no one more devoted to him than myself, to whom he has always shown such warm friendship and encouragement.

For the rest, we remember that what we seek together is the Lord's will, who, in his own good time, will bring all things to completion. Now we live in hope, 'and hope does not disappoint', as the Fathers of the Second Vatican Council quoted from St Paul's letter to the Romans, 'for God's love has been poured into our hearts, through the Holy Spirit who has been given to us' (Rom 5:5). Both Bishop Farquhar and I have experienced the reality of that love in our ecumenical labours, in our common endeavour and in the work that has so much enriched, encouraged and blessed us.

Notes

1. Paul VI, Closing Speech, 8 December, 1965.
2. Pope John Paul II, 'Apostolic Letter on the Preparation for the Jubilee 2000 Year', *Tertio Millennio Adveniente*, n. 18.
3. See, for instance, his encyclical on commitment to ecumenism, *Ut Unum Sint*, n. 3.
4. Ibid., n. 99.
5. Kasper, Cardinal Walter, 'Decree on Ecumenism: Read Anew After Forty Years' in Pontifical Council for promoting Christian Unity, *Information Service*, Vol. 118 (2005/1–2), p. 31.
6. Ibid., p. 32.
7. cf. *Unitatis Redintegratio*, nn. 5, 11, 24; *Ut Unum Sint*, nn. 18, 36, 79.
8. Address to the Conference on the Fortieth Anniversary of the Promulgation of the Conciliar Decree *'Unitatis Redintegratio'* in *The Decree on Ecumenism – Read Anew After Forty Years*.

5 New Churches in Ireland

Adrian Cristea

In the last decade, the fabric of the Irish society has changed profoundly. According to the latest Census results, Ireland's population comprises about 10 percent of non-nationals. Whilst this is not significantly different from our European neighbours, the pace of this change certainly is, and it is probably unique in modern peacetime history. Other countries have faced a much more gradual change in their cultural mix; they had much more time to test the waters. Ireland has been subjected to a somewhat more sudden immersion into the deep end of multiculturalism. Immigrants have contributed to a surge in the memberships of many religious groups in Ireland. Yet the most innovative and dramatic change in Ireland's religious landscape in recent years is not the participation of immigrants in mainline Churches, but rather the birth and spread of immigrant-led religious groups.

The 2006 Census lists twenty-six religions including atheists, other stated religions, no religion and not stated. It also shows a percentage change between the two last censuses, 2002 and 2006. It is interesting to note that among the fastest growing religions in Ireland are the Apostolic or Pentecostal, with a growth rate of 157%. The other rates of changes are: Orthodox, 99%; Hindu, 96%; Atheist, 85%; Lutheran, 72%; Muslim, 69%.

Staggering Changes in Dublin

In Dublin City alone the scale of change in the religious landscape is staggering. It is good to give an account of it because the situation in the Dublin City and suburbs religious landscape is very much reflected in most of the large towns in the Republic. The numbers of black and ethnic Churches are continuing to grow as Irish society becomes more multicultural and diverse.

For instance, in Dublin, one church building, Abbey Presbyterian Church, is now home to three other Pentecostal congregations: the French-speaking Congolese, Nigerian and Romanian. The St George and St Thomas Church of Ireland parish is also host to an Indian Orthodox Congregation. In the vicinity there is a Gideon International Ministry Church and a House on the Rock congregation, both meeting in the Royal Dublin Hotel. A little further on in Sean McDermot Street is a Romanian Catholic Church, which is now well established. St Saviour's Parish in Dominick Street is also home to a Croatian Roman Catholic Chaplaincy.

In the popular area of Moore Street there is a Tower of Power International Ministries, and in Parnell Street there is an African Pentecostal Church, as well as a Polish Church. Glasnevin Industrial Estate is home to the largest African Pentecostal Church, the Redeemed Christian Church of God. Glasnevin is also the headquarters of the network of Redeemed Christian Church of God congregations, also known as 'Joy in the Nation', a network of over forty Churches around Ireland. Middle Abbey Street hosts the Chinese Gospel Church of Dublin, and nearby in Marlborough Street the Salvation Army hosts a Lithuanian Bible Fellowship. Not too far from the city centre, in Clontarf, a Kimbanguist French and Lingala-speaking congregation is using the Methodist Church building to pray and worship.

Crossing the river onto the south side of the city, we encounter, alongside the Lutheran congregation, the Korean Evangelical Fellowship in Adelaide Street. In Pearse Street there is a Romanian Baptist Church sharing a building with an Irish Grace Baptist Congregation, and just around the corner in Westland Row there is a Lithuanian Catholic Congregation. The docklands area is home to an Apostolic Fellowship.

Not long ago the Orthodox Community in Ireland was quite small, comprising a Greek Orthodox Church in Arbour Hill and the Coptic Church in Bray. Within a decade things have changed dramatically. There is now a Romanian Orthodox Church in Leeson Park, and nearby in Harold's Cross the Russian Orthodox Church has set down its roots. The Indian Orthodox Church has now a number of parishes throughout the country, as indeed have many other new Churches too. The Orthodox community also has an Antiochian Orthodox Church.

As we move beyond the city centre into the suburbs, and sometimes into industrial estates, we meet new communities struggling to secure adequate accommodation. Among them we encounter black ethnic minority Churches such as the Mountain of Fire Ministries, Christ Apostolic Church International, the Rock of Ages Cherubim and Seraphim Church, the Celestial Church of Christ and the Deeper Life Bible Church. Among other known black ethnic minority Churches there is the Transfiguration Christian Centre and the Word of Life Church. There are also other Churches about which little or nothing is known.

Needs of the New Churches

In 2002 the Irish Council of Churches commissioned a research project into aspects of the religious life of refugees, asylum seekers and immigrants in the Republic of Ireland. Although it may seem like a long time ago, the findings of the research remain just as relevant today, in particular regarding issues around the needs of these new Churches. What has changed, and in a dramatic way, since the research was carried out, is the membership numbers for these Churches, as shown by the percentage changes indicated at the beginning of this paper. The research identified specific needs these Churches have and, in the context of the continuing increase in membership, these needs are becoming even more pressing.

Among the practical needs of the new Churches, and this seems to be right across the spectrum of new Churches, is that of finding a comfortable place of worship. Many of the Churches started in halls and lounges of hotels or the dining rooms of asylum seeker hostels. In some cases, the groups had to move on because hotel

51

proprietors felt there was a conflict between this use of their premises and their license, or because of the level of 'noise'.

Another difficulty faced by the Churches is finance. Due to the increase in attendance, the need to have a bigger space arises and this brings with it the challenge of meeting costs. At times it seems insurmountable, as often large numbers of the members of the Church are not working. Cases of using venues that do not meet the health and safety regulations abound; in some instances, the local Health Boards have closed some of the venues down. This puts great pressure on the leaders, many of whom are not earning a salary.

Despite these difficulties, attendance at these Churches is very high. Religion as a way of life is closely connected to one's cultural expression. The mode of worship is the most recognised symbol of community and nationality. There is freedom and spontaneity when Africans praise God by dancing, playing music and singing loudly. This is often very different to the Irish mainstream Churches!

In practice, the Churches are also deeply involved in the social and personal issues of their members, including the wider issues of migration and residence. The Churches provide a venue for social-ising and socialisation, and a place to come to fight depression and loneliness. Members see each other as a member of a large family. The dead can be mourned and birth celebrated. In short, the Church helps develop some sense of a community in a strange land.

The research also highlights how an audit of membership of Irish mainstream Churches shows clearly that they have only benefited to a limited extent from the influx of Christian immi-grants to Ireland. While some ministers have been very enthusiastic about these 'strangers', and sympathetic towards their integration into the faith community, some of their members have been resistant to the idea. Another reason for the springing up of black and ethnic Churches is the mode of worship that many in the Irish mainstream Churches find strange. Africans feel very comfortable with the Pentecostal style of worship – that is speaking in diverse tongues, dancing, drumming and clapping.

The findings show that many immigrants want to maintain their identity by having fellowship with people from the same culture.

The study also raises the question: why such a proliferation of black and ethnic minority Churches? Visions given by God to start particular ministries were among the main reasons offered by the individuals who started some of the African Churches. Such ministries are located in the hostels of the asylum seekers and membership reflects the diverse nationalities present. It is interesting to note, however, that some of these hostel residents move on to churches in towns where the leaders are from the same ethnic group. This to some extent is a reflection of the problem of tribalism and inter-ethnic relationships in Africa.

Integration and Identity
Many immigrants coming to Ireland already have contacts or have made enquiries not only about the social and economic life, but also about religious life, so that they get an idea about where their own ethnic community worships. For others, where they go to worship depends on their first contact or where they find them-selves living, for example, an asylum hostel. However, a final choice is usually made after becoming conversant with other Churches in the city or town and deciding which mode of worship they prefer.

In his book, *Embracing Difference,*[1] Canon Patrick Commerford eloquently makes the point that the new communities in Ireland have brought with them their own religious identity and that their ethnic Churches also welcome from beyond the ethnic lines indicated by their names, including Irish people. The important role of these Churches in preserving people's identity and homeland connections is also highlighted.

It can also be argued that a significant number of the immigrants who have joined a black or ethnic minority Church may have wor-shipped in a mainstream Church, but have felt that they were not welcomed and accepted, or were labelled and devalued. A situation where some group in a congregation is labelled and looked on as second class citizens does not augur well for integration.

Often, immigrants are perceived as asylum seekers and, worse still, erroneously regarded as second-class citizens. Therefore, their contributions are seen and treated as less valuable. As we all like to be valued and respected, people move on or start a fellowship where they can feel very comfortable and respected for who they are rather than what they are. Considering that most of the new black and ethnic minority Churches are not members of the inter-Church structures, and thus not within the existing networks, there is a growing need to engage in dialogue and to learn about such Churches in the communities in which they are established.

It is in this context of fast-changing religious fabric in Ireland that the Inter-Church Committee on Social Issues, on behalf of the Irish Inter-Church Meeting, successfully secured funding from the government for a Parish-Based Integration Programme. This three-year project's broad objective is to promote practical integration of immigrants based around parishes or local congregations. The project's first year involved developing support material for promotion of local integration parish-based activities, adapting training material for local groups, visiting local parish groups to provide assistance and practical support required for their integration activities. It also focused on assembling best integration practice resource material from the locations that have been leading the way. As it enters into its second year, the project will focus on enhancing its website with case studies and new resources, it will continue to provide assistance to local communities and much needed follow-up and on-going support to those communities already contacted. Feedback from the local parishes and congregations who have already engaged with the project is very positive, all emphasising the usefulness of the key parish integration guidelines devised by the project.

Guidelines for Welcoming Immigrants

The following parish integration guidelines are in essence a set of practical steps for local parishes and congregations to consider implementing in the process of extending a meaningful welcome and hospitality to the immigrants residing within their boundaries:

1. Carefully analyse your local circumstances in order to be able to provide a meaningful welcome to newcomers.
2. The welcoming process should involve everybody, not just the clergy and parish/Church council.

3. Make sure that the external image of your church looks appealing to newcomers of various ethnic backgrounds. Attractive notice boards and information in relevant languages are helpful.

4. Symbols and messages of welcome are important. Stress the universal dimension of welcome and emphasise your church as a church for all nations.

5. Nominate people to welcome newcomers, giving careful consideration to ensure their suitability for greeting people on arrival and helping them feel at home in church. Learn people's names correctly.

6. Use plain English language in services as it helps those with limited language skills to participate more readily. Incorporate elements into worship from the countries represented in the congregation.

7. Choirs, music and praise groups should seek to learn and incorporate hymns or praise songs in languages representing the diversity of the congregation.

8. Occasional shared meals where everyone contributes food can create a focus for working together and sharing cultural heritage. Celebrate national festivals.

9. Use Bible Studies or other such meetings to develop relationships and promote understanding of different perspectives

10. Promote the participation of newcomers in leadership, project teams, etc. Promote a sense of belonging and of being understood and appreciated.

A more comprehensive and perhaps more valuable resource being developed by the project is the drafting of a guidebook for the integration of new immigrants into their local parishes. It is envisaged that this new resource, now at final draft stage, will provide a wider framework for devising the appropriate integration strategies within a local parishes and congregations context. It will illustrate in detail models of best practice using case studies, and make suggestions for their adaptation and implementation into the particular circumstances of local parishes and congregations. The variety of lessons being learned by various Church communities, as they grapple with the problems and opportunities of creating a diverse and integrated community, has much to offer that is of relevance to the wider Irish society as a whole, as well as to other groups within it.

Another priority for the Parish-Based Integration Programme is to provide a focus for coordination and sharing of resources and experiences between the agencies and committees of individual Churches, as well as with the relevant statutory and non-statutory agencies and other bodies dealing with immigrants. This is particularly so since local communities new to addressing integration activities are most likely unaware of existing services and agencies. Therefore, the work of the project involves informing people of the existing services and agencies and helping them make initial contact. This role of the project was put in practice by organising and coordinating a Dublin City Churches focus group with a view to working closely with the ethnic Churches in particular, in order to obtain their perspective on diversity and integration approaches within the development of an anti-racism, diversity and integration strategy for Dublin City. The focus groups were essential to gathering information as to the perceptions, issues and priorities that are most widespread for these communities. The Parish Integration Project brought together representatives of the Roman Catholic, Methodist, Church of Ireland, the Network of Christian Leaders in Ireland, also known as 'Joy in the Nation', the Romanian Orthodox Church, the Indian Orthodox Church, the Presbyterian Church and the Inter-Church Committee on Social Issues.

Black and Ethnic Minority Churches

A different and valuable dimension of this exercise has been to provide a space for both the mainstream and the black and ethnic minority Churches to meet and talk to each other, as well as other stakeholders, on equal terms. Although on an informal basis, relationships between black and ethnic minority Churches are at best limited; the relationships between the mainstream Churches and the black and ethnic minority Churches tend to fare slightly better, as quite a number of mainstream Churches are offering their premises for use as a place of worship and meetings. This is clearly so in Dublin, Galway and Dundalk. The sharing of church premises is an important area in the development of relationships between immigrant Churches and mainstream Irish Churches.

The sharing of buildings can produce tension and friction and it may be required that agreements are worked out clearly. Officially, the only meaningful or recognised relationship that exists at present is between the Cherubim and Seraphim Church and the Irish Council of Churches. The Cherubim and Seraphim Church does not represent the immigrant Churches, nor can it be expected to. Relationships have to be established with other Churches.

Conclusion – A New Dawn

Dialogue and respect for difference are likely to be the way to move forward. There needs to be more understanding between the immigrant Churches and the mainstream Churches. One of the essential areas for more understanding is in the area of attitudes to worship and different theologies about worship itself. Joint services, as has been the case in some towns, may also help.

Being welcomed into the community of the local Church can be a key moment of successful integration for an immigrant; an invitation of a parish extended to another Christian community of different ethnic background can be the crucial point for integrating that community. Encounters with a community of another ethnic background have been inspiring and enriching for many Churches. In many places, Christian Churches have changed and been revitalised due to the influence of black and ethnic communities.

Welcoming others, respecting their differences as positive values and interacting so that they are fully engaged in the community is perhaps a more complex manner of creating a feeling of belonging. We need to put our differences aside and look for something that we all have in common, and that is our unity in Christ, which we must speak about using a language of unity also. We need to acknowledge that it is only a true description of our faith communities when we all speak this language with conviction, and that we really belong to each other and to Christ.

This is the dawn of a new era and the arrival of Christians and Churches from many cultural backgrounds opens the possibility of testing our Christian witness by that of others, of experiencing one another's gifts and sharing our combined resources. Equally, it opens the prospect of local ethnically-based Churches, operating independently without interest in or concern for other Christian communities. Either of these processes is possible, but only one of them reflects the view of the Church or the Spirit of Christ. Which will we choose?

Note

1. Commerford, P., *Embracing Difference* (Dublin: Church of Ireland Publishing, 2007).

6 Methodist/Roman Catholic Relations

Gillian Kingston

Let us always rejoice to strengthen each other's hand.

John Wesley

Introduction

Writing in Dublin in 1749, John Wesley, in his *Letter to a Roman Catholic*, comments:

> You have heard ten thousand stories of us, who are commonly
> called Protestants, of which, if you believe only one in a
> thousand, you must think very hardly of us. But this is quite
> contrary to our Lord's rule, 'Judge not that ye be not judged';
> and has many ill consequences, particularly this – it inclines us
> to think hardly of you. Hence we are on both sides less willing
> to help each other, and more ready to hurt each other. Hence
> brotherly love is utterly destroyed; and each side looking on the
> other as monsters, gives way to anger, hatred, malice, to every
> unkind affection, which have frequently broke out in such
> inhuman barbarities as are scarce named among the heathens.[1]

Some two hundred and sixty years later, we reflect on the present
state of relations between Roman Catholics and Methodists. And,
thus reflecting, we are bound to call to mind those who make this

relationship manifest; those who, in a real sense, *incarnate* the ecumenical venture. High on my personal list comes Bishop Tony Farquhar, long-time friend and co-worker in things ecumenical. I am a cradle Methodist, deeply committed to that way of being church which is Methodist. A lay woman, I value an expression of church which, in a particular way, enables and encourages the ministry of lay and of women. Bishop Tony is a cradle (Roman) Catholic, deeply committed to that way of being church and holding fast to the teaching and discipline involved in belonging to its priesthood.

We are who we are by birth and that, for most, develops into conviction and commitment. Nevertheless, our principle conviction and commitment centres around the person of Jesus Christ, and we must take with utmost seriousness his prayer that we might be one so that the world might believe (Jn 17:20-23). That we may be one, there needs to be progress at grassroots level, structural level and in theological discourse. Bishop Tony and I have been privileged to operate at all three levels – in diocese and circuit, on the Irish Inter-Church Meeting and on international Theological Commissions. This reflection presents the work of the Methodist/Roman Catholic International Commission and seeks to indicate some directions for Ireland, the land we both love the most.

The Methodist/Roman Catholic International Commission

The Methodist/Roman Catholic dialogue was established shortly after the Second Vatican Council. The World Methodist Council, meeting in London in 1966, accepted an invitation to engage in dialogue and the first meeting took place in 1967. This engagement has continued for forty years without break.

The Commission works in a five-year series of meetings, presenting agreed statements simultaneously to the World Methodist Council and to the Vatican. The Council receives each 'with gratitude' and the Vatican acknowledges each by appointing a scholar to comment on the text.

Cardinal Cassidy, speaking to the Conference of the Methodist Church in Great Britain in June 1998, observed that this dialogue:

[H]as been working away quietly (perhaps too quietly!), but steadily. It has been ... like a deepening conversation, in which we have attempted to listen to each other, to find common ground and recognise that there are areas that are not contentious, in order then to look at similarities and differences.[2]

And indeed this dialogue has remained largely unknown in spite of its long and consistent record of tackling some of the more difficult ecclesiological issues.

A Review of the Reports
The first report of the Commission (Denver)[3] was issued in 1971. It sought to establish common ground on non-contentious issues such as spirituality and Christianity in the contemporary world, and then to move on to sensitivities associated with Christian home and family life. Finally, it raised issues which have subsequently emerged as particularly significant in the Commission's work: eucharist, ministry and authority. [4]

While acknowledging their significance, the Commission:

[A]greed to postpone these important questions because it seemed to us fundamentally important to begin, not with our differences and disagreements, but with our agreements and with that fundamental unity without which all our conversations would cease to be conversations between Christians.[5]

The next report (Dublin, 1976) also ranged widely. However, it noted that:

[M]ore than once ... we have been called to recognise our common heritage; not just to put an ecumenical veneer on the otherwise unalterable furniture of our separation, but to discover the underlying realities on which our churches are founded and to which the common feature of our heritage point.[6]

The third report, *Towards a Statement on the Holy Spirit* (Honolulu, 1981), observed that 'Methodists and Catholics repeatedly discover a notable rapport when they speak of spirituality, the life of the Spirit'. The second section of this report, rejoicing in the delicately balanced title, 'The Holy Spirit, Christian Experience and Authority', picked up on what are neuralgic issues for Methodists and Catholics respectively. It outlined the tension between the outcome of the Holy Spirit's role in drawing believers into faith communities and the role of the Spirit in the teaching and disciplining task of the Church.

The fourth report, *Towards a Statement on the Church* (Nairobi, 1986), pointed out that 'we cannot expect to find an ecclesiology shaped in a time of division to be entirely satisfactory'.[7]

Beginning with a broad view of the nature of the Church and narrowing the focus to concentrate on the area of Petrine ministry, the movement was from the more generally agreed to the more generally contentious. Here is stated for the first time the goal of this dialogue: *full communion in faith, mission and sacramental life.*[8]

Seeking, through Scripture and history, to discern a more universal pattern for ministry, the report admitted that:

> [W]e are not agreed on how far this development of ministry is now unchangeable and how far loyalty to the Holy Spirit requires us to recognise other forms of oversight and leadership that have developed, often at times of crisis or new opportunity in Christian history.[9]

The fifth report, *The Apostolic Tradition* (Singapore, 1991), attempted to set out the theological perspectives in which specific questions may be viewed. With the motif of *koinonia* foremost in the ecumenical mind at the time, the working definition of tradition became '*koinonia* in time'. Set in an understanding of 'The Apostolic Faith: its Teaching, Transmission and Reception' it was hoped that ministry might be viewed from a new perspective, that of 'Serving within the Apostolic Tradition'.

It is precisely here that the major issues lie: apostolic succession and the role of bishops in the Church, the nature of ordination and the location of authority in the Church. These are issues which continue to exercise this and other dialogues.

In the sixth report, *The Word of Life: a Statement on Revelation and Faith* (Rio de Janeiro,1996), the Commission was 'looking for commonly acceptable ways of expounding the historical self-disclosure and indeed self-gift of the triune God, focussed in Jesus Christ, the Word made flesh, and brought home to successive generations of believers by the Holy Spirit, released in power at Pentecost'.[10] It sought to consolidate agreement reached thus far and to provide a basis for movement to more contentious issues, observing that:

> Roman Catholics and Methodists share a common concern regarding the Church universal as an expression of communion in Christ. But they differ widely in their beliefs about the means which God has given to attain or preserve this goal.[11]

The seventh report, *Speaking the Truth in Love* (Brighton, England, 2001), turned its attention to issues surrounding teaching authority. The first section stated, in systematic form, what it is possible to agree on concerning authoritative teaching, noting the divergences that remain and the questions one side would like to put to the other; the second section described the practices and understanding of each party in a way readily accessible to the other. It is suggested that those unfamiliar with either or both partners should read this first!

Acknowledging that 'Christ's Church is totally dependent on the free gift of God's grace for every aspect of its life and work',[12] the report reflected on how this grace may be channelled and through whom:

> [S]ome of our remaining differences centre on whether and how a means of grace may be 'guaranteed' or 'trustworthy'. Catholics ask Methodists how and by what criteria they verify that a particular means is a trustworthy channel of God's grace. Methodists ask Catholics whether the idea of the guaranteed quality of a sacrament takes full account of the weakness, limitations and sinfulness of the human beings called to be agents of God's grace ...[13]

The eighth and most recent report, *The Grace Given You in Christ* (Seoul, 2006), indicates in its subtitle something of the 'cumulative' methodology of this dialogue – 'Catholics and Methodists *further* reflect on the Church.' [14]

The opening chapter reflects on the perceptions each partner has had of the other: though there was sometimes genuine understanding, mutual evaluations were more often:

> [C]oloured by the religious, social and political conflicts which have generally characterised relationships between Protestants and Catholics, and they were fed by mutual ignorance, defective understandings or partial views of each other.[15]

However, the changes that came with the Second Vatican Council resulted in 'a shift from polemics to dialogue, from accusation to respect and from ignorance to trust.'[16]

The second chapter notes that Methodists and Catholics are agreed on much that constitutes church. The serious divergences concern ministry and these include 'a precise understanding of the sacramental nature of ordination, the magisterial role of the episcopate in apostolic succession, the assurance asserted of certain authoritative acts of teaching, and the place and role of the Petrine ministry'.[17]

Using the language of 'gift'[18] and acknowledging that 'the Holy Spirit is the true giver of all gifts,'[19] the third chapter highlights 'the gifts we truly have to offer each other in the service of Christ in the world.'[20]

Acknowledging that there is a difference of starting place, 'Catholics have an instinct for the whole and an emphasis upon the confident actions of the Church as Church, while Methodists have an instinct for the individual and an emphasis upon the assurance that each individual has'[21] and, further, that 'Catholics tend to think first of *apostolic succession* and Methodists of *mission*,'[22] the report considers what gifts we might each offer the other.

Among those which Methodists might offer Roman Catholics are:[23]

- The role of lay people in both preaching and the decision-making process of the Church;
- A concept of ministry which includes lay people and which includes women among the ordained;
- A characteristic ethos in worship and spirituality, expressed often, though not exclusively, through the hymns of Charles Wesley.

The gifts Roman Catholics, in their turn, might offer Methodists include:[24]

- An articulated ecclesiology, with a sense of continuity both in space and in time;
- The Petrine ministry, offered as a service of love and unity;
- Those doctrines, which at the Reformation became obscured rather than reformed of excess and which, at the Second Vatican Council, were re-articulated; among these understandings of the Eucharist and of the priesthood.

Noting Pope Benedict's words that 'Concrete gestures that enter hearts and stir consciences are essential, inspiring in everyone that inner conversion that is the prerequisite for all ecumenical progress',[25] the final chapter of the report seeks to 'earth' the agreement reached during forty years of dialogue. This section is carefully structured in terms of the declared goal of full communion in faith, mission and sacramental life. Outlining a number of principles and proposals for closer working together, the Report allows that:

> The practical proposals outlined in this chapter do not exhaust the possibilities for closer collaboration. Nevertheless, (they) constitute a comprehensive set of concrete gestures that will assist our two communions as we journey towards the next stage on the way to our full visible unity.[26]

And in Ireland?

But does this have any impact on the local ecumenical scene? If we are to be honest, no! An issue faced by every theological dialogue is that of reception: how are new insights and understandings to be conveyed to the faithful so that their lives and discipleship may be informed and enriched?

The Seoul report notes a number of national Methodist/Roman Catholic dialogues – in Great Britain, New Zealand and the United States. What are the possibilities for establishing such a dialogue in Ireland to confer on matters of common interest, theological and otherwise? An officially constituted national dialogue might go some way towards breaking the proverbial glass ceiling. The international reports might provide a starting point for discussion. Archbishop Diarmuid Martin, speaking at the annual Conference of the Methodist Church in Ireland in June 2004, raised the possibility – it is time to *real*-ise that thought.

The latter part of the 2006 Seoul report has indicated a programme for closer relationship, at different levels within our Churches, including at parish and circuit level. The challenge is to leadership at diocesan and district level to promote, encourage and enable such relationship building.

There are, of course, non-theological factors which militate against such drawing closer. Apart from the baggage of history, there is extreme disproportion in numerical strength. In the Republic of Ireland, those declaring themselves to be Methodist are some 0.3% of the population, while those declaring themselves to be Roman Catholic are 86.8%. In Northern Ireland, the respective figures are 3.5% and 40.0%.[27]

It is of the nature of the case that minorities tend to know rather more about majorities than majorities know of the minorities among them. There is therefore a considerable task involved in simply getting acquainted, of learning each other's history, language and ways of worship. The Methodist Church has produced a booklet entitled *Methodist Belief* [28] precisely to inform those who want to learn about 'the people called Methodist'.

Together we rejoice in a new, if sometimes tentative, climate of rapprochement among Christians on this island. Nevertheless, both

Methodists and Roman Catholics are aware of a swelling tide of apathy and indifference towards faith matters among people traditionally associated with the Churches. It is a complicated scene and it becomes further complicated as we encounter increasing numbers of those of other world faiths establishing themselves among us. If we know little enough about each other, what do we know about those of other belief systems? And yet that too is complicated, as we use this more 'distant' issue to avoid consideration of the issues among ourselves.

Roman Catholics and Methodists need to take cognisance also of the fact that everywhere we encounter each other in this country, we are in the company of others – Christian, people of other faiths and of no faith. The challenge is how to celebrate what we share in Christ without seeming to exclude others with at least some of whom we may be at other stages of relationship. However, as the Chinese proverb says, 'the longest journey starts with the first step', so let's get going!

Conclusion

Welcoming his Excellency Philip McDonagh[29] to the Holy See, Pope John Paul observed that:

> The message of the gospel cannot be separated from the call to a change of heart; neither can evangelisation be isolated from ecumenism and the promotion of fellowship, reconciliation and openness to others, especially to other Christians. May the initiatives of all those who seek peace and reconciliation be blessed by God's grace and bear fruit for the children of tomorrow.[30]

The task is far from finished. However, Methodists and Roman Catholics are working, praying, witnessing together in a way that would not have seemed possible forty years ago. We should not, therefore, be discouraged, we are in a very different place to that from which we started – and it is a better place.

Welcoming his Excellency Francis Campbell[31] to the Holy See, Pope Benedict made that very point:

I encourage all those involved in this work never to rest content with partial solutions but to keep firmly in view the goal of full visible unity among Christians which accords with the Lord's will.[32]

John Wesley concluded his *Letter to a Roman Catholic* with some rules for relationships such as ours:

In the name, then, and in the strength of God, let us resolve first, not to hurt one another; to do nothing unkind or unfriendly to each other, nothing which we would not have done to ourselves. Rather let us endeavor after every instance of a kind, friendly, and Christian behavior towards each other.

Let us resolve secondly, God being our helper, to speak nothing harsh or unkind of each other. The sure way to avoid this is to say all the good we can both of and to one another; in all our conversation, either with or concerning each other, to use only the language of love to speak with all softness and tenderness, with the most endearing expression which is consistent with truth and sincerity.

Let us, thirdly, resolve to harbor no unkind thought, no unfriendly temper, towards each other. Let us lay the axe to the root of the tree; let us examine all that rises in our heart, and suffer no disposition there which is contrary to tender affection. Then shall we easily refrain from unkind actions and words when the very root of bitterness is cut up.

Let us, fourthly, endeavor to help each other on in whatever we are agreed leads to the kingdom. So far as we can, *let us always rejoice to strengthen each other's hands in God.*[33]

It is the task and privilege of friends to strengthen each other's hands in God. We rejoice with Bishop Tony in our companionship on the way to that unity, which is both God's gift and will for his Church: 'We are strangers no longer but pilgrims together.'[34] The words of Charles Wesley, the three hundredth anniversary of whose birth we have just celebrated,[35] encourage us along that way:

Christ, from whom all blessings flow,
Perfecting the saints below,
Hear us, who Thy nature share,
Who thy mystic body are.

Never from Thy service move,
Needful to each other prove;
Use the grace on each bestowed,
Tempered by the art of God.

Love, like death, has all destroyed,
Rendered all distinctions void;
Names and sects and parties fall;
Thou, O Christ, art all in all.[36]

Notes

1. Wesley, J., 'A Letter to a Roman Catholic' (July 18th 1749), par. 1, in T. Jackson (ed.), *The Works of the Rev. John Wesley, A.M. Sometime Fellow of Lincoln College, Oxford*, 3rd rev. ed. (London: John Mason, 1856), Vol. 10.
2. The text of this address was reproduced in the *Epworth Review*, Vol. 25 (1998/4), pp. 13–22.
3. With the tacit assent of the Roman Catholic side, the documents have assumed popularly the name of the location in which the relevant World Methodist Council has met and its date. The Denver (1971) and Dublin (1976) reports had no formal title, but subsequent reports are as follows: Honolulu (1981), *Towards a Statement on the Holy Spirit*; Nairobi (1986), *Towards a Statement on the Church*; Singapore (1991), *The Apostolic Tradition*; Rio (1996), *The Word of Life*; Brighton (2001), *Speaking the Truth in Love*; and Seoul (2006), *The Grace Given You in Christ*. All documents will be cited by the city followed by the paragraph number.
4. These issues have emerged as priorities in almost every dialogue, e.g. ARCIC.
5. Denver, par. 100.
6. Dublin, par. 17.

7. Nairobi, par. 22.
8. Ibid., par. 20.
9. Ibid., par. 29.
10. Rio, par. 1.
11. Ibid., par. 130.
12. Brighton, par. 49.
13. Ibid., par. 61.
14. My italics.
15. Seoul, par. 11.
16. Ibid., par. 39.
17. Ibid., par. 92.
18. See Pope John Paul's Encyclical Letter on Commitment to Ecumenism, *Ut Unum Sint*, n. 28: 'Dialogue is not simply an exchange of ideas. In some way it is always an "exchange of gifts"'. Cf., Vatican II's constitution on the nature of the Church, *Lumen Gentium*, n. 13.
19. Seoul, par. 97.
20. Ibid.
21. Ibid., par. 99.
22. Ibid., par. 101.
23. Ibid., par. 114–120.
24. Ibid., par. 128–135.
25. First Message of His Holiness Benedict XVI at the end of the Eucharistic Concelebration with the members of the College of Cardinals in the Sistine Chapel, 20 April, 2005, §5.
26. Seoul, par. 163.
27. On a global level, there are approximately one and a half billion Roman Catholics to seventy-four million Methodists. The figures above come from the 2006 Census in the Republic of Ireland and the 2001 Census in Northern Ireland respectively.
28. *Methodist Belief*, Methodist Church in Ireland, 2003.
29. Ambassador of the Republic of Ireland to the Holy See, 2004–2007.
30. Address delivered on September 5, 2004.
31. Her Britannic Majesty's Ambassador to the Holy See since 2005, Francis Campbell, is from Newry.
32. December 23, 2005.

33. *Letter to a Roman Catholic,* p. 17. My emphasis.
34. Collect for Christian Unity, *Methodist Worship Book 1999* (Peterborough: Methodist Publishing House, 1999).
35. Charles Wesley, 1707–1788.
36. *Hymns and Psalms,* 764 (London: Methodist Publishing House, 1983).

7 The Community of Protestant Churches in Europe

Rev. Prof. Cecil McCullough

I have known Bishop Farquhar for many years since he worked as a chaplain in Queen's University, Belfast and have always admired his ability to cross boundaries and communicate at every level. His many achievements and accomplishments in Belfast and the whole island of Ireland are very well known and admired. In the wider world, however, it will probably be for his ecumenical work, particularly in the World Alliance of Reformed Churches' (WARC) Roman Catholic dialogue that he will be best known, and so in this short tribute I want to describe one important ecumenical dialogue, which is part of the European Reformed tradition: the Leuenberg Agreement, and subsequent Leuenberg Fellowship based on it, and to consider, very briefly, its relevance for the Ireland of today.

My first acquaintance with the Leuenberg Fellowship was when I was appointed by the Presbyterian Church in Ireland to represent our Church at the Fourth General Assembly of the Leuenberg Fellowship in Vienna in 1994. On the flight from Belfast to Vienna, one question kept surfacing. What was the possible relevance of such an Assembly for the Churches in Ireland? After all, the Assembly was being held in Vienna, in the heart of Europe; its language would be mainly German and the main issues dealt with would be those of Continental Europe. Moreover, it represented, as

Professor Grosser, the great French Humanist, said in his keynote address on the first working day, an historical 'truce' to stop the name-calling which had gone on for centuries between Churches, which had come from the Reformation. That name-calling, however, was hardly a major issue in Ireland where there has been plenty of name-calling, but it has been carried out across a rather different divide.

As the Assembly progressed, however, answers began to emerge. For a start, while German was the dominant language and while at times when issues were being hotly debated, especially in the smaller groups, those whose mother tongue was not German were at a decided disadvantage (as happens to those whose mother tongue is not English at many other major conferences and assemblies), an excellent interpretation service meant that all could take part. More importantly, however, the large numbers of delegates from minority Churches in the former Eastern Europe and South America, the invitation to the European Methodist Churches to begin the process of joining the Fellowship and the decision to begin conversations with the Anglican Communion brought the work of the Fellowship much closer to home for those living both in Ireland and Britain.

How the Leuenberg Fellowship Came About

The background to the Leuenberg Agreement was the scandal of the division within Churches coming out of the Reformation, where even in small villages there was no table or pulpit fellowship between Lutheran and Reformed Churches. Many developments had prepared for the signing of the Agreement in 1973.

Inside Germany from the nineteenth century onwards, the phenomenon of United Churches *(Unierte Kirchen)*, where in particular Lutheran and Reformed Churches came together, for example, in Hamburg, kept the issue of Church unity to the fore in Protestant German theological thinking. Thinking about Church unity was further encouraged by the famous Barmen theological declaration in 1934, which had involved the coming together of Lutheran, Reformed and United Churches in a common witness in the Church/Nazi struggle of that time. Then in 1947 there was a

Church gathering in Treysa, Germany, which called for a 'binding theological conference on the doctrine of holy communion' which would allow Churches to enter into table fellowship. Six rounds of talks took place between 1947 and 1957, and the Arnoldshain Theses on Holy Communion were adopted. While this was a theological breakthrough, it apparently had little practical effect on life on the ground. Finally, between 1968 and 1970, further talks were held within Germany between Lutherans and Reformed Churches and these talks established the 'Theses on Church Fellowship' of May 1970. As a result, the Churches were ready for the next step – the drawing up and signing of the Leuenberg Agreement.

Outside Germany, conversations between the Lutheran World Federation and the World Alliance of Reformed Churches had been going on from 1955, culminating in the third round in 1969 in Leuenberg. These conversations showed that it ought to be possible to work out an agreement, which would later be acceptable to the Churches and on which table and pulpit fellowship could be based in all of Europe.[1]

The actual agreement was made in 1973 and by April 1976, sixty-nine out of the eighty-eight Churches involved had already signed it and sent their agreement to the Faith and Order Commission. Since then over one hundred Churches have signed it. The precise figure varies as some member Churches unite and others join. The Churches are also limited to Europe, with four Latin American Lutheran Churches that have strong links with Europe. The European Methodist Church joined in 1996.

The position of the Nordic Lutheran Churches is rather unique – only the Norwegian Church has signed the Concordia (in 1999); the rest have not signed it, but participate in every way in the activities of the Fellowship. There are two reasons for this: firstly, their state constitution (particularly in Denmark) makes it difficult to enter into fellowship with non-Lutheran Churches. Secondly, theologically, their doctrine of fellowship must involve a process of growing together into full structural Church fellowship and, as we shall see, this is a long-term goal of the Churches of the Leuenberg Fellowship, not a prerequisite for joining it.

Reconciled Diversity

The basic model for the Leuenberg Agreement is unity in *reconciled diversity*. The Churches declare Church fellowship 'in loyalty to the confessions of faith which bind them or with due respect for their traditions. Through this we can recognise each other as churches if in our fundamental confessions we agree on the one truth of the Gospel yet express it in a diversity of forms'. Hence the main thrust of the agreement is on our core beliefs, the teaching of the gospel. The first main section of the Agreement (after the historical preamble) is entitled 'The Common Understanding of the Gospel', which is subdivided into Justification, Preaching, Baptism and the Lord's Supper. The Agreement goes on to deal with the mutual doctrinal condemnations within the reformed family in the time of the Reformation era and concludes:

> Wherever these statements [Doctrinal statements about the gospel etc.] are accepted, the condemnations of the Reformation confessions in respect of the Lord's Supper, Christology, and predestination do not affect the doctrinal position. This does not mean that the condemnations pronounced by the Reformation fathers are irrelevant; but they are no longer an obstacle to church fellowship. There remain considerable differences between our churches in forms of worship, types of spirituality, and church order. These differences are often more deeply felt in the congregations than the traditional doctrinal differences. Nevertheless, in fidelity to the New Testament and Reformation criteria for church fellowship, we cannot discern in these differences any factors which should divide the Church.

Clearly such a process and final statement is open to the criticism that it is merely living with and thus ratifying the status quo. If this criticism is to be met, then the Leuenberg Agreement must be seen as the start of a process rather than its completion. This process was seen to be two-pronged – doctrinal and practical – and was guided by a series of Assemblies (Sigtuna, Sweden, 1973; Driebergen, 1981; Strasburg, 1987; Vienna, 1994; Belfast, 2001; and Budapest, 2006) and between the Assemblies by an executive committee (now called a council). They monitor ecumenical progress on the ground, set up regional groupings and also design and set up continuing theological conversations and studies.

Ecumenical Progress

If the signing of the Leuenberg Agreement did not result in increasing Church fellowship leading towards unity on the ground, it would be a failure. However, it has been successful in many areas of Germany where it is particularly relevant. There have been more difficulties and, perhaps, less success in other European countries. In Ireland and the British Isles it has never been perceived as the chief ecumenical instrument in promoting unity or co-operation between Presbyterians, Methodists, Episcopalians and Lutherans. This is because of several factors: the Lutheran Church is very small in Ireland; the Presbyterians and the Methodists already have a long tradition of Church fellowship, with joint congregations and joint teaching of theological students in Union Theological College and Edgehill Theological College for the past fifty years; the Methodists and the Church of Ireland have already developed their own covenant, which is part of the covenant between Methodists and the Anglican Church in the British Isles. Nevertheless, the Leuenberg Agreement does provide an important model for ongoing conversations.

Conversations With Other Church Families

On the European level, ecumenical consultations have been held with the Churches involved in the Meissen Agreement and the Porvoo Agreement in 1995, 2004 and 2005, the Orthodox Churches of the CEC in 2002 and the European Baptist Federation (EBF) in 2000, 2002, 2003 and 2004. These have lead to a greatly increased understanding of each other and of the difficulties in the way of deepening fellowship between the different Churches and full recognition of each other's ministries.

Regional Groups

An important role of the executive committee is to oversee regional groups. Two of these have been particularly active in the past years:

the South East Central Europe Group and the North West Europe Group. They have met for theological discussion of contemporary topical issues and have produced papers, which have been commended by the executive and successive General Assemblies of the Leuenberg Fellowship. It is difficult to see the value of a regional group in Ireland and Britain, as there are already very good and well-established forums for the ecumenical sharing of discussion on topical issues, but in the context of South Eastern Europe in particular, the group has played a very important role in encouraging ecumenical dialogue.

Doctrinal Studies
On the doctrinal side, much energy has been expended on writing doctrinal papers on various topics. The CPCE (Community of Protestant Churches in Europe), as it is now called, has published these papers under titles such as, *The Two Kingdoms, The Lordship of Christ, Baptism, Freedom and Responsibility, The Church* and *The Relationship between the Church and Judaism.* Present consultations are on the topics of 'The Protestant Understanding of Ministry, Ordination and Episkopé' and 'Scripture – Confession – Church'. The documents are, in my opinion, of an excellent standard and a first-class resource for all Churches. There are, however, several problems associated with them.

While they are published in a very distinctive series by Lembeck Verlag, Frankfurt, distribution, especially in Great Britain and Ireland, has been very poor. Even for those who know them and want to use them it is exceedingly difficult to get hold of them.

Moreover, because the documents are highly technical and theologically accurate, they are hardly bedtime reading for the average Church member (even when they are translated into high-standard English, which has not always been the case). Successive executive meetings have tried to get round this by suggesting publishing a 'popular' version, but quickly realised that such popular versions, which would miss the nuances that had been so carefully written into the text, could be problematic.

A second question raised by some is the amount of energy expended on them, perhaps to the neglect of the ecumenical consultations. While many (and I would count myself among those) see great ecumenical value in formulating the Protestant contribution to, say, the theology of the Church, and would say it is foundational for any further ecumenical work, others see it as a diversion from what they consider to be the only show in town – bilateral discussions between the large world federations, such as the World Alliance of Reformed Churches, the Lutheran World Federation, the Orthodox Church, the Anglican Communion and the Roman Catholic Church.

Consultations

Finally, the CPCE has organised consultations on contemporary international topics such as 'Training for Ordained Ministry in the Leuenberg Church Fellowship', which took place in 2003 in Berlin, and a 'Consultation on the challenges of migration and flight', which resulted in the Liebfrauenberg Declaration (2004). They have been particularly geared to specialist groups, such as theological professors or social workers and politicians, and have served as a forum for the exchange of information and expertise within the specialised areas.

Conclusion – Relevance in Ireland

The Community of Protestant Churches in Europe is part of a continuing process. Work continues in the area of doctrine, in representing the Protestant Churches in Europe, in ongoing conversations with the Orthodox Church, the Porvoo and Meissen Churches and the European Baptist Federation and in developing Church fellowship locally throughout Europe. It is one contribution, among many others, towards breaking down misunderstandings among Churches. It is very conscious that it is part of a much wider picture and recognises that it must be very careful not to hinder other dialogues that are taking place between Churches of the CPCE and Churches outside it. Its members feel, however, that its basic model of 'unity in reconciled diversity' is a useful one, which can contribute to the Church's attempts to break down the walls of partition between us and reverse the trend of mutual hostility and growing apart which has been characteristic of much of the Church's development in the past.

What of its relevance in Ireland? Certainly, as we have seen, much of the original context in which the Fellowship developed is not replicated in Ireland. However, its under girding model of 'unity in reconciled diversity' can make an important contribution to healing divisions among the Churches in Ireland. It involves having respect for each other's different traditions and deeply held convictions and yet, at the same time, making the effort to find our common convictions and to build on those. It does not involve forcing anyone to give up a cherished tradition but rather to ask the question: is this tradition of necessity Church-dividing? It goes on to pose the two questions: can we, on the basis of our commonly held beliefs, recognise each other's ministries? Can we then, on the basis of our understanding of the gospel, deepen our fellowship through listening to each other and through shared theological reflection and common witness in today's world? This attitude of mind serves, in my view, as a good foundation on which to base ecumenical discussion.

Also, perhaps the model of unity in reconciled diversity is one which is of value in our fraught political arena as well. The application of the model would involve the recognition of our shared values, acceptance of our differing traditions and a determination to advance along the road of reconciliation, through dialogue and study and through joint political action to meet the practical needs of the country. In that way, enough trust would hopefully be built up between former enemies to facilitate the growing together of society and the fulfilment of all the hopes which have been raised in the past few years.

Note

1. For an excellent account of these talks see Lukas Fischer's article, 'A History of the Leuenberg Agreement' published in 1998 on the twenty-fifth anniversary of the signing of the Agreement. It can be found at http://warc.ch/dt/erl3/11.html.

8 The Orthodox Church in Ireland 2008

Rev. Godfrey O'Donnell

Eastern Christian Orthodox parishes did not exist in Ireland before 1969. A small number of Russian émigrés arrived shortly after the 1917 Bolshevik Revolution, among them Nicholas Couriss, later to be Ireland's first resident Orthodox priest.

The life of Fr Nicholas reads like an adventure story with all the sweep of a Russian novel. He came from the minor nobility and was an officer in the Imperial Guard in St Petersburg, the capital of Russia at the turn of the century and the city where the imperial family resided. In the winter, the great families of Russia would give receptions at their houses and the officers of the Guard would be invited. Nicolas fell in love with one of the daughters of the house, but it was a hopeless love. Her family was among the most powerful in the country and had played a significant role in Russian history. Part of his duties included accompanying the royal family to the courts of Europe, including Vienna and Berlin. Then came the Great War in 1914 and he found himself in the west fighting Germans. Eventually the Revolution broke out and he fought on the Tsarist side until he and many others like him had to flee the country penniless. In Constantinople he met the woman to whom as a young guardsman he had lost his heart. They married and eventually made their way to England.

After World War II, with the growing power of the Soviet Union, England instructed her diplomats to start learning Russian, and a house was rented in Wicklow for the purpose. The future Fr Nicholas was sent there as a language teacher. Some Irish diplomats also attended, including soon to be Irish government minister, Conor Cruise O'Brien. Nicholas' marriage produced a son, but sad to say he died early of diphtheria. Some time after this his wife died and he developed arthritis. Therefore, his position in such a large house became untenable. After this it was decided by some of the Russian community in Ireland that Nicholas should be sent to an Orthodox seminary in the USA to train for the priesthood, and return to serve the Russian Orthodox in Dublin. He was at this time about seventy years old.[1] In 1969, the parish of our Lady's Holy Protection was established by the Russian Orthodox Church Outside of Russia (ROCOR) – who chose not to maintain links with Moscow after the Revolution, but are now again part of the Moscow Patriarchate since May 2007 – with Father Nicholas as priest.

A number of Irish were received into the Church. Venues for the Liturgy, according to Gregory Strachan, one of the parishioners, included The Seamen's Institute, Trinity College Chapel, St Andrew's Red Cross home in Dundrum, and The Haven, a Masonic home for the elderly in Clonliffe – all demonstrating how difficult it was to find a permanent worshipping space. Eventually, because of his frail health, the community created a chapel in a house that friends lent Fr Nicholas for the duration of his life. From 1971–1973 he was assisted by Fr Michael Beaumont, a University College Dublin lecturer in English literature and priest of the Moscow Patriarchate. Fr Nicholas died in August 1977, and with him the tiny house chapel at 45a Pembroke Lane.

Several hundred Orthodox, including Greek and Greek Cypriots, had settled in Ireland by the early 1950s. The first Greek Church was consecrated in 1981 at St Mary's, Mary Street, Dublin. Fr Ireneu Craciun, who was just finishing his doctorate in theology in Maynooth, was appointed priest in charge. In 1986 the building was declared unsafe. A mendicant period ensued, temporarily using Gonzaga College Chapel and the 'Tin Church' in Ranelagh. A permanent building was found at Arbour Hill and it was consecrated in 1994. A sign of development is to be found in the ordination in 2007 of Father Tom Carroll, an Irishman, to the priesthood for the Greek Church.

The late 1990s saw an influx of people from Eastern Europe. The Russian Church (Moscow Patriarchate) began its services in 1999. Later came the Romanian Orthodox, the Antiochian Orthodox, Georgian Orthodox, the Malankara Jacobite Syrian Orthodox and the St Thomas Indian (Malankara) Orthodox Churches.

The Antiochian Church has two centres in Ireland, one in Belfast in the Collins Room, St James Church of Ireland, with Fr Irenaeus du Plessis as its priest. The second centre is in Dublin in St Joseph's School for the Visually Impaired Chapel, with a newly ordained Irish priest, Fr David Lonergan. The centre in Belfast runs a three-year diploma course in applied Orthodox theology. A fourth year can lead to an MTh accredited by Balamand University in the Lebanon. It is a distance learning programme, with occasional residency courses. There are fifteen students enroled in the full programme at the moment.

The Georgian Church came into being in July 2006 with the appointment of Fr Malkhaz Kumelashvili to Ireland by the Catholicos-Patriarch Ilia II. The present community consists of two to three hundred members and worships in the chapel of the Dominican College, Cabra, through the good auspices of the Roman Catholic archdiocese of Dublin.

The Romanian Church came into being with its own priest in October 2000 when the first priest, Fr Calin Popovici, arrived in Ireland from Cluj-Napoca, sent by Metropolitan Iosif of the Romanian Orthodox Metropolis of Western and Southern Europe, which has its headquarters in France. For the first six months Fr Calin lived with an Irish family perfecting his English and pursuing an MA programme in theology at the Milltown Institute. Through this he made the beginnings of many Irish friendships. During this time he made contact with the Romanian Association and some of its members, and also with some Romanian families scattered throughout the country. From January 2001, Sunday worship began in Belvedere College Chapel in the centre of Dublin, courtesy of the Jesuit Fathers, and 2004 marked the first Orthodox ordination of an Irishman in the parish. Fr Godfrey O'Donnell was raised to the priesthood on 15 February by Metropolitan Iosif in Belvedere Chapel to be the assistant priest. Around the same time, Fr Calin Popovici had to return to Romania for family reasons and Fr Calin Florea, also from Cluj-Napoca, took over from him as parish priest.

With the expansion of numbers, there followed a search for larger premises, and in June 2005 the Church of Ireland gladly made available their building at Christ Church, Leeson Park, Dublin to the Romanian Orthodox community. On 9 April, 2006, Deacon Fr Viorel Hurjui was ordained priest with responsibility for a newly created second parish in Cork. Monthly liturgies are offered in Galway, Limerick, Mullingar, Kildare and, more recently, Belfast. This year another Romanian priest, Fr Raul Simion, arrived to help with the communities in Galway and Limerick.

The Romanian Church have been practicing some seven years in Ireland. As of now there are two constituted faith community parishes: one worshipping at Christ Church, Leeson Park, Dublin, and catering for perhaps one and a half thousand members scattered around the city. The second worships courtesy of the Presentation Sisters at the school chapel, South Douglas Road, Cork.

With the accession of Romania and Bulgaria into the EU, there has been a notable increase in the Dublin Church community. Numbers at the church have been averaging over three hundred over the last six months. The vast majority of the community are still immigrants with little English, and initially without many (or any) family connections or friends in Ireland. The centres, therefore, still wear different hats. On the one hand, the church is a social centre providing links and human support. It is also an information centre providing information about social welfare, health, doctors, lawyers, government agencies and immigration problems. Though most members are now part of the EU, there are still those Romanians from the Republic of Moldova who find it extremely difficult to obtain visas.

The Romanian Church is in the throes of consolidating its Dublin and Cork parishes and communities, and establishing a Sunday school for its children in Dublin. There are now English classes for adults and music classes for children. This last Lent an adult catechesis programme was started up for members in Dublin. In all this, basic religious education remains a concern. At present, there are other centres in Galway, Limerick, Mullingar, Kildare and Belfast, but these are small as yet (perhaps fifty members in each), though with obvious potential. There is still a need for constant help with regards to getting in touch with the wider Orthodox community in Ireland. Other Churches have been very helpful along the way, letting the Romanian Church know if they come across Orthodox who find themselves isolated. This is simple, straightforward ecumenical work, not to be despised!

The Russian Church began its services in 1999 with monthly liturgies at the Greek Church, Arbour Hill, but subsequently moved to premises in Harold's Cross, Dublin in 2002, which it had since acquired from the Church of Ireland (Anglican). Under the direction of its Dean, Fr Michael Gogoleff, and Parish Priest, Fr George Zavershinsky, it now includes other worship centres in Cork, Galway and Waterford. The Church also runs a Russian school for its children.

The Oriental Orthodox Churches

The Oriental (or pre-Chalcedonian) Orthodox Churches survive to this day in Syria, Lebanon, Israel, Egypt, Ethiopia, India and Armenia. As so often happens in history, theological differences can be exacerbated by cultural and national pressures. This was true of Egypt and Syria, both predominantly non-Greek in language and background, and both beyond the pale of the Byzantine Empire during the fifth century. They resented the power of Greek Constantinople both in religious and political affairs, and found themselves unable to accept the Council of Chalcedon (451) and its Greek terminology about the 'nature' of Christ. Both sides wished to affirm the same basic truth about Christ the Saviour – that he is fully divine and fully human, and yet he is one and not two. Had it not been for the non-theological elements, the 'non-Chalcedonian' and the 'Chalcedonian' groups might have reached an accommodation after the Council.[2] Sadly, our separateness over the centuries seems to have more to do with terminology than theology.

Copts (Egyptian Christians) started arriving in Ireland in the late seventies. Most of the Copts in Ireland are medical doctors, who originally came here to study but decided to stay. In more recent years, Copts have come with more diverse backgrounds, to pursue careers in business, IT and science. In September 1979, the first Coptic liturgy in Ireland was celebrated in the chapel of the Rotunda Hospital by a Coptic priest from London, who used to come once every six weeks. This practice continued from 1979 to 1990. In December 1990, Pope Shenouda III appointed for the first time a priest dedicated to Ireland, Scotland and Wales, Fr Axios Anba Bishoy. He was later consecrated as Bishop Antony and established a large number of churches in Scotland, north-east England and its affiliated areas. Fr Axios bought the church in Bray in 1993. In July 1997, Fr Athanasius George was ordained for the altar of the Church of St Mary and St Demiana, and to be the first priest appointed solely for Ireland. Since then the number of Copts has increased in the country and there are now communities in Cahir, Galway, Cork, Tralee and Belfast. Nationalities in the Church include Egyptian, Eritrean, Ethiopian, Irish, English, American, Iraqi, Palestinian, Sudanese, Polish, Latvian, French and Lebanese.

Since the mid-seventeenth century, the Syrian Patriarchate has included an autonomous Church in India, now called the Malankara Jacobite Syrian Orthodox Church. This Church has found a home at St Paul's, Arran Quay in Dublin, under its vicar, Fr Jobymon Skaria. There are further parishes in Galway, Waterford and Belfast, each with its own priest, and growing centres in Dundalk and Tallaght.

The roots of the St Thomas Indian Orthodox were planted nearly six years ago by a small Orthodox community from the southern part of India, Kerala. A goodly number of its members came to Ireland to help out in the nursing profession. It started as a prayer group and later formed itself into a congregation. In December 2006, it was officially declared a parish by the diocesan Metropolitan Dr Thomas Mar Makarios, who sadly died recently;

eternal memory. Fr Koshy Vaidyan was appointed Vicar and President. The Indian Orthodox diaspora in Ireland is scattered over a number of centres. There is a second parish in Belfast under Fr George T. Two other priests, Fr Varghefe Maniambrayil stationed in Athy and Fr Ninan Kurakose in Cavan, look after congregations as well as prayer groups in Waterford, Cork, Sligo and Drogheda.

The Orthodox Mission in Ireland

The mission of the Orthodox Church in Ireland is seen as fulfilling the instruction of Christ our Saviour to 'go and make disciples of all nations, baptising them in the name of the Father, and of the Son and of the Holy Spirit, and teaching them to obey everything that I have commanded you' (Mt 28:19-20) since he 'desires everyone be saved and come to knowledge of the truth' (1 Tm 2:4). In Ireland, this will be primarily done by continuing to preach and serve the diaspora of Orthodox presently living and working in Ireland, other Orthodox who have no spiritual home and those others, particularly Irish, who might be drawn to the Orthodox faith. For us it is not about getting into competition with other Christian Churches, it is about sharing the riches of our tradition and an invitation to 'come and see'.

An Ecumenical Approach

The Metropolitans and Archbishops of the Orthodox Church are keen that the Orthodox Churches here in Ireland reach out to other Churches. Realistically, the most that can be done for now, given where most members of the Orthodox Churches are situated in Ireland, is to encourage them to get a taste of other worshipping Christian communities through visiting other Churches from time to time during the year, and of getting a growing number of their members, especially the younger people, involved in common Dublin Council of Churches (DCC)/Irish Council of Churches (ICC) events. For instance, there was good involvement with the Lutheran Church in setting up the Advent Walk of Light in the Greater Leeson Street area. Members also got involved in the hosting of the inaugural Dublin Church Unity service last year, as well as participation in other Church services. A number of the Churches are members of the Irish Council of Churches and two are members of the Dublin Council of Churches. Still, there obviously remains much to do in educating some members ecumenically. As well as this, it is important to establish a link with other Orthodox brothers and sisters – Antiochian, Coptic, Georgian, Greek, Indian, Romanian, Russian and Syrian. This is not a given. The first full meeting together was held in early March this year: six of the eight Churches sent representatives. Last but not least, the Dublin Council of Churches honoured the Romanian Church by electing Father Godfrey as their Chairperson! It is nice to think that an Orthodox priest played some small part in facilitating the Roman Catholic archdiocese of Dublin integration into what was until recently a mainly Protestant group, but now with a growing Orthodox presence.

There is no doubt that the ecumenical work that some of the Orthodox Churches have been involved in has somewhat raised the visibility of Orthodoxy in the country. There has been a growing number of invitations to speak about Orthodoxy to other Church groups, as well as invitations to publish.

The Future

Much more needs to be done to mediate an active Orthodox presence among the Irish. Peter Sutherland, Irish international banker, Chairman of BP and Goldman Sachs International, with a portfolio in many other organisations including government, trade and economics, had this to say in a recent interview mapping out a path for the Irish economy:

> Migration is now a new challenge. It is also a difficult issue to handle as we can see from experience elsewhere in Europe. If Ireland is to have a 5 per cent growth rate over the next few years, we will require a huge number of additional migrants coming into this country. The inward migration figures in the last years for Ireland and Spain are unique in Europe. Such migration can ultimately lead to issues unless carefully handled. We have only just begun to grapple with them in the sense that

we still have no holistic policy approach to it. Over 10 per cent of our workforce are non-Irish today and if the growth rates were to continue as they are, we are going to find that escalating at a very remarkable pace over the next five or six years. It is hard to see how, with strong growth, it can be stopped. Nor should it be from a moral point of view ... Also we have got free movement within the EU and it's a relevant part of what the EU is. So we still have to grapple with issues like the arguments for assimilation as opposed to multi-culturalism, and so on. We have not even begun to think in depth about these issues. While I am not as optimistic about the future as some, nor am I apocalyptic. I think we have very real challenges here in terms of our cost structure and our over-dependence on the construction sector.[3]

While much of what he says is positive and hopeful for immigrants, Romanians and Bulgarians still do not have full freedom of movement and rights in the EU, especially in those countries outside the Schengen area, namely Ireland and the UK. The decision of the Irish government to not allow Romanian nationals access to the labour market is a big issue. Also, the fact exists that those who do not have a residency permit and/or work permit are now in a state of limbo, as the immigration legislation does not apply to them and they do not have full EU freedom of movement rights. The situation in Northern Ireland seems to be similar. The Romanian and Bulgarian Orthodox in Ireland feel hard done by. Visas continue to be a problem for some of the other Orthodox too.

A fair number of the Orthodox coming to Ireland are economic immigrants looking to improve their lot, help their family and/or extended families back home. Many will only stay in Ireland for a limited period of time. But some have already decided to stay on in the country, even to the extent of applying for citizenship. These people and their children are going to create a rather different Church over time, both in terms of language and culture, and we have to prepare for that.

Staring us in the face is the inevitable problem of the multiplicity of jurisdictions already surfacing in our small country. We

Orthodox have to learn to live and work together, sooner rather than later, and stop duplicating the Lord's work. We have limited resources; we should use them wisely. Above all, we have to move on from ethnicity in our juridical organisation. There is no doubt that many of the Eastern Europeans who have come to our country have enriched us with their tradition of the Christian faith. The Orthodox way has brought another aspect of Christianity to offer their fellow Christians. However, for it to ultimately find roots and new life in Ireland, it has to discover its Irish expression. That has always been the understanding of the Orthodox mission as it attempts to enculturate in a new country.

Metropolitan John Zizioulas of Pergamon, one of the most eminent of contemporary Orthodox theologians, responding to the conferring of an honorary doctorate on him at the Institut Saint-Serge in Paris in February last, made this point, among others, about the contribution of western Orthodox theology to the Orthodox world in general:

> I will start with the *future of eucharistic ecclesiology*. Linked to this question, a certain number of important problems are starting to face the Orthodox Church. Eucharistic ecclesiology implies that there is only *one* local Church in each place, united in *one* eucharist, under *one* bishop. We all know that this principle is not respected. The very fact creates a contradiction between theology and life, theory and practice. If this situation continues much longer, eucharistic ecclesiology will become a joke. The problem of the Orthodox diaspora must be solved without delay. The Orthodox Church in the West can no longer be organised along national lines. It must be developed starting with the *local dimension*, and not nationality.[4]

It seems to me that the Holy Spirit is saying loud and clear to us that we need more priests, priests from our different countries and Irish priests open to the melting pot of our different cultures, to learning from one another and, perhaps equally important, learning also from the wider Irish Church, Roman Catholic and Protestant.

Notes

1. See Shanley, P., *Cathair Na Mart*, Vol. 17, 1997; and Strachan, G., *Orthodoxy in Ireland: An Article for the Sixth Anniversary of the Opening of the First Orthodox Church in Dublin* (Unpublished).
2. See Ware, T., *The Orthodox Church: New Edition* (London: Penguin Books, 1997), pp.28–29.
3. 'So how did we get here?' Words by Peter Sutherland, interview by Paul Sweeney, *Irish Times Business Magazine* (Dublin: February, 2008) p.20; see also Sweeney, P., *Ireland's Economic Success: Reasons and Lessons,* chap. 2: Peter Sutherland (Dublin: New Island, 2008) pp.24–25.
4. De Pergame, Métropolite Jean (Zizioulas), *Service orthodoxe de presse,* no. 326, March 2008, pp.27–28.

9   *The Global Christian Forum: The Framework of an Ecumenical Breakthrough*

Mgr John A. Radano

The Global Christian Forum (GCF) met November 6–9, 2007 in Limuru, Nairobi, Kenya.[1] It involved two hundred and forty-five participants from seventy-two nations and six continents. It included representatives of a broad span of Christian communities: the historic Protestant Churches, the Catholic Church, the Orthodox and Oriental Orthodox Churches, the Pentecostal Churches, the broader Evangelical movement, and other Christian Churches and communities. The gathering, which met under the theme, 'Our Journey with Jesus Christ the Reconciler', was unprecedented. As its 'Message to Brothers and Sisters in Christ throughout the World' described it, 'Here in Limuru we have experienced an historic breakthrough, gathering globally as never before'.

'Gathering Globally as Never Before' – The Elements of an Ecumenical Breakthrough

This meeting of the Global Christian Forum represented a certain type of ecumenical breakthrough in several ways. First, it has been described as the most representative gathering of Christian families ever. On the one hand, it included representatives of those historic Churches which, in general, have been involved in the modern ecumenical movement. Among these are the Orthodox, Oriental

Orthodox, Catholics, Anglicans and a broad range of Churches stemming from the Reformation. On the other hand, it included representatives of Pentecostal and Evangelical Churches and movements, many of whom have not participated in structures of the modern ecumenical movement. They often have reacted negatively to those structures, such as the World Council of Churches (WCC). They often have refused contacts with the Catholic Church or other mainline Churches. Those of their members who, for one reason or another, have judged some of the latter as not truly Christian, have sometimes tended to treat them as targets of evangelisation resulting in more conflict. With this background, it is interesting to note that organisations represented at Nairobi included the World Council of Churches, the World Evangelical Alliance and leaders of the Pentecostal World Conference. Some of these would not have been present together at a meeting before, nor would some Pentecostals have taken part in a meeting involving Catholics.

Second, the breakthrough came in the 'configuration' of the representatives there. It constituted something new. The meeting was designed in a way that roughly 50 per cent of the participants came from 'mainline Churches' and 50 per cent from Pentecostal/Evangelical movements and Churches. This pattern had been followed in the much smaller regional meetings which preceded Nairobi and had been organised as part of the evolving Forum process. They took place in Asia (2004), Africa (2005), Europe (2006) and Latin America (2007). Previous meetings in the USA in 2000 and 2002 had gradually made the decisions to undertake these regional meetings and to organise them in the configuration just mentioned. Thus the configuration of participants at Nairobi, with roughly half from mainline Churches and half from Pentecostal/Evangelical Churches and movements, represents the largest meeting in which these two sizeable constituencies – which some conveniently designated as 'Ecumenicals' and 'Evangelicals' – have taken part according to that arrangement.

Thirdly, while there were some in lectures or presentations made at Nairobi to help focus on themes, much time was spent in small groups allowing the participants to hear each other's personal witness to the Christian faith. This methodology of stressing the sharing of personal experiences of faith rather than formal ecumenical dialogue, used also in the regional meetings leading to Nairobi, was effective in helping to break down stereotypes, which had developed as a result of centuries of separation up until current times.

Symbolically, the representatives of mainline Churches and those of Pentecostal/Evangelical Churches, in many cases for the first time, sat across the table from one another, face to face as equal partners in a search for the reconciliation of Christians in keeping with the theme of the meeting: 'Our Journey with Jesus Christ, the Reconciler'. They prayed together, they learned about each other's faith commitment, they listened to one another's journeys of faith. They constructed together a message to Christians all over the world. They outlined possible steps forward for the GCF process. All of this represents an ecumenical breakthrough. Now it requires efforts to see whether this experience will foster deeper ecumenical activity, including dialogue, to resolve Church-dividing ecumenical issues.

But how did this come about? What was the anatomy of this ecumenical breakthrough?

Steps Leading to the Global Christian Forum
In the process of describing the various factors leading to this ecumenical breakthrough, one can look both to the recent steps leading to it, and to the more remote background as well. For while this GCF in a true sense is a new ecumenical initiative in the twenty-first century, it is also in a number of ways the product of a long history of ecumenical developments over the last century.

Immediate Steps
As to recent history, the Global Christian Forum was born out of the reflection process in the World Council of Churches during the 1990s concerning a 'Common Understanding and Vision of the World Council of Churches' (CUV). It was seen that even if the World Council of Churches succeeded in clarifying its own common understanding and vision, there are still millions of Christians, especially Pentecostals and Evangelicals, whose communities are

neither member Churches of the WCC, nor in many cases participants in the various structures of the modern ecumenical movement. WCC General Secretary, Dr Konrad Raiser, therefore suggested the need for some type of new forum of Christian Churches and ecumenical organisations, in which those Christians might participate as equal members with others. The WCC, the Catholic Church, the Orthodox and other historic Christian Churches might each have a place in this new forum with Evangelicals and Pentecostals. It would not begin with any preconceived structure or constitution. Rather the theory was that, as needs became clear, any structure that they might initiate would be the joint responsibility of all those sitting at this new 'table', so to speak. With time this process came to be called the Global Christian Forum.

The WCC began to consult ecumenical partners about the feasibility of a new type of forum, and an initial proposal was developed at a WCC-sponsored meeting in August, 1998. This proposal was brought to the WCC's Eighth Assembly in Harare, Zimbabwe in December 1998, where the idea was given significant attention.[2] The Assembly supported the continuation of consultation towards developing the idea of the forum. Thus the idea emerged within the WCC and was given significant support by the most authoritative voting body of the WCC.

Next, the WCC began to interest other partners in this idea. These included the Vatican's Pontifical Council for Promoting Christian Unity (PCPCU). During 1997–1998, the WCC was in direct contact with the PCPCU on this matter. General Secretary Raiser sent a representative to Rome to visit the PCPCU to explain the idea and seek support. The PCPCU accepted the invitation to participate in exploring this idea with the following understanding. It wished that priority be given first to settling the reorganisation of the WCC resulting from the CUV process (the PCPCU had earlier submitted to the WCC its own reflections on the CUV process), and that the forum should be a channel for strengthening the goal of visible unity, which is stated in the World Council of Churches' constitution, even if this goal was not expressly stated in the purposes of the proposed forum. Also, this new forum should meet a need not being met by any existing organisation. The Pontifical

Council for the Promotion of Christian Unity hoped that this forum initiative could draw into the one ecumenical movement those many Christians not at present directly involved in the current structures of the modern ecumenical movement.[3] The PCPCU was represented at the first WCC consultation on this in August, 1998. The PCPCU has been represented on the Continuation Committee appointed thereafter, which was given responsibility to explore the idea further and eventually to guide the process over the years.

Other ecumenical partners became involved. The Continuation Committee included Hubert van Beek, a WCC staff person who became Secretary of this process. He continued as Secretary after his retirement and the WCC continued to support him in this position. At the beginning, participants on the Continuation Committee also included representatives of the Moscow Patriarchate, the YMCA, the South African Council of Churches, the Syrian Orthodox Patriarchate, the Pontifical Council for Promoting Christian Unity and the Anglican Communion. A Pentecostal, Dr Mel Robeck, participated in a personal capacity. All of these have continued to be represented on the Continuation Committee, except the South African Council of Churches (though the SACC has continued its support of the process). After the second meeting in the USA in 2002, it was agreed to invite four additional participants to the Continuation Committee to strengthen Evangelical and Pentecostal representation together with women and youths. One of these was Dr George Vandervelde, a member of the theological Commission of the World Evangelical Alliance. Later, Wesley Granberg-Michaelson, General Secretary of the Reformed Church in America, was appointed by the WCC as its representative on the Continuation Committee. To avoid possible obstacles to the participation of some groups, the Continuation Committee has proceeded, with the approval of all involved, as an independent body, and not under the authority of the WCC or of any ecumenical organisation or confessional family.

The Conference of Secretaries of Christian World Communions (CS/CWCs) became another important partner in this process. Meeting annually since 1957, this conference brings together the general secretaries, or their equivalent, of virtually all the major

Christian World Communions. It is organised in an informal way. It includes communions stemming from the Reformation and others, which developed in the centuries after the Reformation. Orthodox participants include representatives of the Ecumenical Patriarchate and the Moscow Patriarchate. The Catholic Church is represented by the Secretary of the Pontifical Council for Promoting Christian Unity. The World Evangelical Alliance has participated. A Pentecostal leader takes part in a personal capacity. This CS/CWSs is therefore a widely representative body.

The CS/CWCs heard reports about the forum developments at each annual meeting and consistently gave its support. Of special significance, the Conference decided to hold its 2007 annual meeting in Nairobi, on days just following the Global Christian Forum (November 10–11). It did this with the intention that the general secretaries of CWCs could be present at the GCF meeting. This meant that at Nairobi, leaders of a variety of Christian World Communions at a very high level of authority would participate in the Forum. The World Evangelical Alliance also scheduled its international council meeting in Nairobi on dates adjacent to the GCF meeting. This insured the presence at the Forum of Evangelical leaders of a very important global Evangelical organisation.

Furthermore, as the Global Christian Forum process continued, over the years it began to involve other ecclesiastical groups and ecumenical bodies. As mentioned above, early in the process, a small initial meeting was organised in 2000 at Fuller Theological Seminary in Pasadena, California, USA to test the idea with some Pentecostal and Evangelical leaders, in order to gauge if there was any interest. The venue was chosen because Fuller is one of the best-known Evangelical seminaries in the world. When it was clear that there was an interest, another larger meeting took place in 2002 at the same location. Representatives of important confessional and ecumenical organisations were already involved in these early meetings. One result of the 2002 meeting was the decision to hold a series of regional consultations on different continents to foster growth of the forum concept in different parts of the world. These would be convened under the general theme of 'Jesus Christ – our Journey with him'. There would be at least two keynote speakers at each meeting, one from the Pentecostal/Evangelical side, the other from among those whose Church or organisation was historically involved in ecumenism.[4]

The first, in Hong Kong in 2004, was organised in consultation with the major Asian ecumenical body, the Christian Conference of Asia (CCA), the (Catholic) Federation of Asian Bishops Conferences (FABC), the two of which had already been involved in close ecumenical contacts during the previous decade, and the Evangelical Fellowship of Asia (EFA). As a result of this meeting, the three groups made an informal commitment in principle to form a Continuation Committee for Asia.

The regional meeting for Africa took place in 2005, in Lusaka, Zambia. Some of the organisations involved included the All Africa Conference of Churches (AACC), which is the continental ecumenical body, the Association of Evangelicals in Africa (AEA) and the Organisation of African Instituted Churches. Local and regional Catholic organisations and a number of Christian World Communions, such as the Lutheran World Federation, the World Alliance of Reformed Churches and others, sent representatives also.

At the European meeting in 2006 in Warburg, Germany, the Council of European Catholic Bishops' Conferences was represented along with other regional organisations and CWCs. The regional gathering in Latin America was held in Santiago, Chile, in 2007, with the assistance of the Latin American Council of Churches and including representatives of the Catholic Bishops' Conference of Latin America (CELAM), as well as other regional groups of Evangelicals and CWCs.

Some sixty to seventy people took part in each of these meetings. These regional meetings were pivotal because they not only brought this forum idea to the attention of people in different parts of the world, but they did so with the assistance of some of the main ecclesiastical confessional bodies and CWCs, as well as ecumenical organisations. Most of those mentioned, and more, would also be represented at the large meeting of two hundred and forty-five people in Nairobi in 2007, which was both a culmination of the forum process thus far and the event which would point to its future.

More Remote Steps: Streams of the Ecumenical Movement

While the origin of the Global Christian Forum in the World Council of Churches and the various meetings from 1998–2007 constitute the immediate steps leading to the event in 2007, there were, of course, also remote steps, found in the various streams of the ecumenical movement shaped over decades.

There is an important statement in the message of the 2007 Nairobi meeting, which alludes to the broader ecumenical movement. Expressing the commitment to press on in promoting ever greater understanding and cooperation among Christians, it says that 'in doing so, we build on the basis of many ecumenical, inter-confessional and other historic initiatives to overcome divisions in the Christian family. We do not seek to replace these efforts'.

In the background of this gentle and factual statement, there was a debate at Nairobi over the use of the word 'ecumenical'. Some participants asked that the word 'ecumenical' not appear in the message. This position did not prevail. But this debate in fact represented one of the major tensions at the very heart of the meeting in November 2007, and of the whole Global Christian Forum process itself. The debate reflected a basic reason for initiating and developing the forum process. For many of those Christians not directly involved with the modern ecumenical movement or its structures, such as those in the newer Pentecostal and Evangelical movements, the word 'ecumenism', in their perception, had come to represent compromise of truth or subscribing to a 'liberal theology', which somehow rejects aspects of apostolic faith or giving less attention to evangelisation. This attitude towards the word ecumenism was true also for some Orthodox, rooted in experiences resulting from life under communist regimes. Much of this was the result of stereotypes, which developed due to lack of contact with the structures of the ecumenical movement or with mainline Churches involved in the ecumenical movement. This was precisely why the new space provided by the GCF and the particular methodology it used – that of emphasising personal contact – and providing a lot of time in the meetings for participants to listen to the faith journeys of other

Christians was necessary. Thus, the Global Christian Forum process has taken place for almost a decade. There was a need to build bridges between these groups that had not been in touch with each other before.

But the remote background of the Global Christian Forum was precisely the modern ecumenical movement itself, which many say started especially with the 1910 World Mission Conference in Edinburgh, Scotland. Other movements such as the Faith and Order and Life and Work took shape around the same time. These led to the establishment of the World Council of Churches in 1948. The Second Vatican Council, 1962–1965, gave impetus to the Catholic Church's involvement in the movement.

The WCC, in its continuing efforts to serve its member Churches and the ecumenical movement, has also made space for the voices of non-member Churches, including Evangelical and Pentecostal voices. For example, the official report of the WCC's Sixth Assembly at Vancouver, Canada in 1983 indicates that there were Evangelicals at the Assembly. In fact, they put their names to an open letter which said that Vancouver's spiritual and biblical orientation had 'challenged stereotypes some of us (Evangelicals) have had of the WCC'. The letter took a strong line against fringe groups that had picketed delegates and distributed 'scurrilous' literature. While offering some criticisms of the Sixth Assembly, the letter called for active participation in the ecumenical movement and challenged 'that all too popular Evangelical heresy' – that the way to renew the body of Christ is to separate from it and relentlessly criticise it.[5]

The Official Report of the Seventh WCC Assembly (1991) in Canberra, Australia, includes 'a letter to churches and Christians Worldwide from Participants who share Evangelical Perspectives'. The letter was also signed by some Pentecostal participants.[6] The Canberra Assembly also formulated resolutions concerning relationships between the WCC and Pentecostals.[7]

The Official Report of the Eighth WCC Assembly (1998) at Harare also includes 'A Jubilee Call: A Letter to the WCC by Evangelical Participants at Harare'.[8] The Harare Assembly also asked the WCC and its member Churches to seek 'new forms of relationships with Evangelicals in the spirit of the CUV', and approval was given to the formation of a 'new joint working group with Pentecostals and a number of tasks were outlined for it, including broadening the range of the existing dialogue between the WCC and Pentecostals and "initiating studies and exchange on issues of common interest including controversial issues"'.[9] After the Seventh Assembly in 1991 had formulated resolutions concerning relationships between the WCC and Pentecostals, a number of consultations and other contacts had already taken place in the 1990s.[10] Harare continued these contacts by establishing and approving, as just mentioned, the formation of a WCC–Pentecostal joint working group.[11] One of the factors influencing this WCC development was the international Pentecostal–Roman Catholic dialogue, which had already been in progress for twenty-five years.[12]

The international dialogue between the Catholic Church and the Classical Pentecostals, which has continued without inter-ruption since 1972, represents the longest and most fruitful international dialogue between a mainline Church and the Classical Pentecostal movement. The Catholic–Pentecostal international dialogue has now had five phases, producing five reports. Something of the range of topics covered can be seen even in the titles of the last three. The report of the Third Phase was entitled *Perspectives on Koinonia* (1990); that of the fourth phase was *Evangelisation, Proselytism and Common Witness* (1993); and that of the fifth was *On Becoming a Christian: Insights from Scripture and the Patristic Writings With Some contemporary Reflections* (2007). The latter especially broke new ground in that, for the first time, besides biblical reflection, Catholics and Pentecostals reflected together and extensively on patristic materials relating to the theme.

In more recent years, other Christian World Communions have engaged Classical Pentecostals in bilateral dialogue. The World Alliance of Reformed Churches and Classical Pentecostals held a first phase of dialogue from 1996–2000, publishing a report entitled *Word and Spirit, Church and World*. This dialogue is ongoing. The Lutheran World Federation's Ecumenical Institute at Strasbourg and Classical Pentecostals have held preliminary consultations in recent years working towards a formal dialogue.

Concerning international bilateral dialogue involving Evangelicals or Evangelical Organisations, the Evangelical–Roman Catholic Dialogue on Mission (ERCDOM), held during 1978–1984, is the first between representatives of the Evangelical movement and the Catholic Church. On the Catholic side, the dialogue was coordinated by the Vatican's Secretariat for Promoting Christian Unity. On the Evangelical side, there was no international organisation acting as sponsor, and the participants came on their own authority. A decade later, the Catholic Church and the World Evangelical Alliance engaged in dialogue (1993–2002), publishing a report entitled *Church, Evangelisation and the Bonds of Koinonia* (2003). This was the first international dialogue between the Catholic Church and a global Evangelical organisation.

Another development important for the GCF process was the dialogue between the World Alliance of Reformed Churches (WARC) and the Organization of African Instituted Churches, held between 1998–2002. This was the first international dialogue between WARC and the OAIC, and it published a report in 2002.

There have been bilateral dialogues, especially since Vatican II, between Churches that have participated in the modern Ecumenical movement – for example, dialogues between the Catholic Church and the Orthodox Church and between the Catholic Church and various world communions stemming from the magisterial reformation. Gradually, dialogues and consultations have been taken up between the Churches involved in the modern ecumenical movement and the more conservative Christian World Communions, such as the Baptist World Alliance and Seventh Day Adventists, many of whose member Churches have had significant questions about the WCC or other ecumenical structures, or have had in some places a history of deep conflict with the Catholic Church or other mainline Churches. As such, they have a lot in common with the Evangelical Churches and movements, which participated in the Global Christian Forum. These contacts also form part of the background to the GCF. Thus, the World Alliance of Reformed Churches and the Baptist World Alliance held conversations from 1974–1977. The Lutheran World Federation and the Baptist World Alliance held conversations between

1986–1989. The Anglican Communion and the Baptist World Alliance held conversations from 2000–2005. The Catholic Church and the Baptist World Alliance held a first phase of conversations in 1984–1988 and began a second phase in 2006, scheduled to be completed in 2010. A Seventh Day Adventists–World Alliance of Reformed Churches dialogue took place in 2001.

Other contacts could be cited, but these previous contacts involving Pentecostals and Evangelicals and the various bilateral conversations just mentioned form an important part of the ecumenical background to the GCF process over the years before the Nairobi meeting in 2007. Though something new such as the Global Christian Forum still had to take place in order to contribute to breaking down barriers of separation and challenging stereotypes, much had been done before and during the years of the GCF process that had already begun to create new relationships. This was noted during various GCF regional meetings and in the Message from Nairobi.

Conclusion

The period just after Vatican II might be seen as a new stage in the ecumenical movement, because from that time Pentecostal and Evangelical Churches and movements began to participate more in the ecumenical movement, either in bilateral dialogues or in contacts with the World Council of Churches. Their participation brought new challenges. The wide range of traditions present at the GCF in Nairobi, 2007, marks a certain culmination of the GCF process that had developed during the previous eight years. It also reflects a high point in that new stage of the ecumenical movement.

The question now is to determine in what direction the GCF should go. One direction concerns fostering a fresh reception of the reports of theological dialogue in which Pentecostals and Evangelicals have been involved over recent decades. These reports could now be seen anew by more members of all those constituencies since, through the experience of the Global Christian Forum, many have now seen other Christians in a new light. Hopefully there will be new opportunities for the important theological work already found in dialogue reports to be seriously considered again by some, and perhaps for the first time by others. The convergences and agreements already achieved offer opportunities for deepening the mutual understanding, which the GCF has promoted.

Another direction might be to find new ways to invite GCF participants into closer or direct contact with structures of the modern ecumenical movement, such as the World Council of Churches or others.

More ecumenical contacts need to take place. The desire to foster response by Christians to Christ's prayer for the unity of his disciples must continually be nourished. The Global Christian Forum is in a position to contribute to this.

Dedication

It is a pleasure for me to contribute these reflections on the Global Christian Forum to this festschrift in honour of Bishop Anthony Farquhar. My closest contact with him has been to work with him in the third phase of the international Reformed–Catholic dialogue, 1998–2006, at which he served as Co-Chairman. His dedication to that dialogue was one of the factors that brought it to a successful conclusion, resulting in an important report entitled *The Church as Community of Common Witness to the Kingdom of God* (2007). That report can significantly deepen mutual understanding between Catholics and Reformed.

The Global Christian Forum is a more recent development in the ecumenical movement. But it requires for success the same dedication necessary for the success of every aspect of ecumenism: the deep dedication that Bishop Farquhar has brought to the international Reformed–Catholic dialogue and to every other ecumenical context in which he has worked.

Notes
1. Hereafter, I will often refer to this meeting as 'Nairobi'.
2. *Together on the Way: Official Report of the Eighth Assembly of the World Council of Churches.* Diane Kessler (ed.), (Geneva: WCC Publication, 1999). See the many references to 'Forum of Christian Churches and Ecumenical Organizations'.

3. 'Global Christian Forum', in *Joint Working Group Between the Roman Catholic Church and the World Council of Churches, Eighth Report,* Geneva and Rome 2005, (Geneva: WCC Publication, 2005), pp. 6–7.

4. A very useful history of the Global Christian Forum is presented in Sarah Rowland Jones, 'The Global Christian Forum: A Narrative History', in *Global Christian Forum: Transforming Ecumenism,* Richard Howell (ed.), (New Delhi: Evangelical Fellowship of India, 2007).

5. *Gathered for Life: Official Report VI Assembly World Council of Churches, Vancouver, Canada, 24 July–10 August 1983,* David Gill (ed.), (Geneva: World Council of Churches and Grand Rapids: Wm. B. Eerdmans, 1983), p. 17.

6. 'Evangelical Perspectives from Canberra', in *Signs of the Spirit: Official Report Seventh Assembly of the World Council of Churches, Canberra, Australia, 7–20 February, 1991,* Michael Kinnamon (ed.), (Geneva: WCC Publications and Grand Rapids: Wm B. Eerdmans, 1991), pp. 282–286.

7. *Signs of the Spirit,* p. 108.

8. 'Responses from Evangelical Participants', in *Together on the Way: Official Report of the Eighth Assembly of the World Council of Churches,* Diane Kessler (ed.), (Geneva: WCC Publications, 1999), pp. 265–271.

9. 'WCC Membership and Relationships', in *Together On The Way,* p. 153.

10. 'Relations with Pentecostal Churches' in ibid., pp. 167–168.

11. Ibid., p. 168.

12. Ibid.

10

The Promise of 'Growing Together in Unity and Mission' for the Development of Anglican–Roman Catholic Relations

Dame Mary Tanner

C oming out of our own corners, getting to know others and building friendships across ecclesial divides are prerequisites for the reconciliation of Churches. Bishop Tony Farquhar, in whose honour this essay is penned, is someone who knows that and lives it. I am thankful that I have had the privilege of working with Bishop Tony, particularly in the context of Anglican–Roman Catholic relations, where I have learnt from him and experienced his gift of friendship.

This essay seeks to tell the story of the provenance of the recently published Agreed Statement from the International Anglican Roman Catholic Commission for Unity and Mission (IARCCUM) – *Growing Together in Unity and Mission* (GTUM), a story in which Bishop Tony has played an important part. The significance of the Agreed Statement is better understood when something is known about its provenance and its status. The story is worth telling because it illustrates some important things about Anglican–Roman Catholic relations over the past forty or more years, revealing something about the closeness as well as the fragility of our two Communions today.

Vatican II – 1982: 'Heady Days'
We need to go back to the heady days after Vatican II when the Roman Catholic Church came enthusiastically into the ecumenical

105

scene. No Church since then has given so much energy or resources, or produced so many outstanding ecumenical theologians as the Roman Catholic Church. Bishop Tony is an example of one who has sought to deepen ecumenical relations on a local, regional and international level, not least of all by his co-chairmanship of the International Roman Catholic–Reformed dialogue and his membership of IARCCUM.

Following on the end of Vatican II, Archbishop Michael Ramsey made an historic visit to Pope Paul VI – two saintly and ecumenically-committed leaders meeting in that collision of hopes and dreams for the future re-union of our two Communions.

At the end of the visit, their Common Declaration recognised the new atmosphere of Christian fellowship between the two Communions. They spoke of their intention to set up a theological dialogue to face the theological issues between us and also to promote practical contacts and collaboration. In other words, Anglican–Roman Catholic relations were to develop along a twin track – theological/doctrinal conversations and practical collaboration – where convergence in faith and convergence in life were to go hand in hand.

This twin track approach was filled out in much greater detail by a small Commission in its *Malta Report* of 1978.[1] The Commission too envisaged that advances in theology and lived relations would belong together. The Commission saw Anglican–Roman Catholic relations advancing in step-like fashion. New stages of relatedness would be established on the basis of agreements and convergences in faith and would be expressed practically in new forms of shared life and mission. A first stage had already been entered into on the visit of Archbishop Michael Ramsey to Pope Paul VI when they publicly acknowledged the degree of faith Anglicans and Roman Catholics already shared. This first stage was to be followed by further stages of 'phased *rapprochement*' on the way to the goal of 'organic union'. Each new stage would be celebrated and officially endorsed by the two Communions.

Things got off to a very good start. Agreed statements on Eucharist, ministry and authority were swiftly produced by the first Anglican–Roman Catholic International Commission (ARCIC).[2]

At each stage the documents were offered to the Churches for study and comment and large numbers of laity and clergy were involved in responding to the reports. The Commission responded to points raised in a series of Elucidations. The result of the conversation between the Commission and the faithful was that there was a genuine enthusiasm and expectancy that there was soon to be an official change in Anglican–Roman Catholic relations. If the two Communions did share a common faith about the Eucharist, the ministry and ordination, and were converging in their understanding of authority, then surely eucharistic hospitality as well as the recognition, if not reconciliation, of ministries would follow? It was a time of expectancy and genuine excitement, not least of all among those in inter-Church families, who live in an intense way the pain of the separation of the Churches.

1982–2000: 'Things Began to go Wrong'

But then things began to go wrong. The heady days were over. First, the reaction of the Congregation for the Doctrine of the Faith to *The Final Report of ARCIC* appeared to some to be hard line, looking for identity of language with that used in the Roman Catholic Church.[3] Official observations noted the lack of reference to the doctrine of transubstantiation. But to look for conformity with Roman Catholic language seemed to some to miss the point of ecumenical conversation and ecumenical documents, which attempt to express together afresh the faith of the Church for today in language that is not identified with one side in a polemical past. In such re-expression neither partner should expect to find a repetition of its own language.

Secondly, between 1986 and 1988 the Anglican Communion was in the process of discussing the consecration of women as bishops, in response to a request coming from the Episcopal Church in the USA. By the 1988 Lambeth Conference, all the provinces had studied the matter and an Archbishops' Commission had laid out the theological and ecumenical arguments for and against. The Commission set two possible courses of action before the bishops at the Lambeth Conference. The bishops did not settle the matter once and for all. Their Conference Resolution stated that if a province were to consecrate a woman as bishop, convinced that there were no theological reasons against that and that the mission in its particular context required such a move, then other provinces would remain in the 'highest degree of communion possible'. The matter would continue in an 'open process of discernment and reception', in the Anglican Communion and also in the wider Church. This development in the ministry of the universal Church presented difficulties for the Roman Catholic Church and for some Anglicans.

Thirdly, enthusiasm among some Anglicans for ARCIC had waned because by the 1988 Lambeth Conference, there was still no official response from the Roman Catholic Church to the work of ARCIC, only the critical response of the CDF. It seemed to onlookers that there might be a tussle going on between the Pontifical Council for Christian Unity and the CDF. Anglicans began to ask whether there was any longer in Rome a serious interest in the Anglican Communion. Moreover, many knew that the ordination of women, and now the possible consecration of women as bishops, would inevitably complicate the relationship and make any advance in relations difficult.

The loss of enthusiasm for ARCIC meant that when the Lambeth bishops came to articulate the mind of the Communion in *The Final Report of ARCIC,* they responded only to the first and not the second question that had been put to the text. The first question was whether the *Final Report of ARCIC* was 'consonant with the faith of Anglicans/Roman Catholics'. The second question asked each Communion to consider what 'concrete steps' might be taken on the basis of the agreements in faith. The linking of the question about theological agreement with practical steps in life was wholly faithful to the original vision of Archbishop Michael Ramsey and Pope Paul VI, and faithful to the intention of the *Malta Report.* But when the Vatican made its official response it, too, like the Anglican bishops, failed to answer the second of the two questions, the question about praxis. The dynamic of harnessing the articulation of growing agreement in faith together with deepening relations in life had been abandoned, or forgotten.

More theological talk was commissioned in a mandate given to a new ARCIC Commission by the Pope and Archbishop Robert Runcie on the occasion of the Pope's visit to Canterbury, movingly captured in the photo of the two leaders kneeling and praying at the tomb of Thomas a Beckett. Over the next two decades, ARCIC II produced a series of important agreed statements on salvation and the Church, the Church as communion, morals, authority in the Church and the role of the Blessed Virgin Mary. There was some study made of these texts but no formal response was called for. Neither was there any widespread conversation between the Commission and the clergy and laity of either Communion, as there had been in the case of ARCIC I. Perhaps there was a fear that too many hopes had been raised in the first round of ARCIC conversations that had proved impossible to fulfil. Perhaps the implied criticism of the processes in both the Roman Catholic Church and the Anglican Communion was a cause of anxiety, or perhaps it was simply genuine unclearness about how to respond to this relatively new ecumenical process of theological dialogue, a process in which neither Church had been engaged before. What was clear by the late 1990s was that the original vision of theological dialogue and deepening relations going hand in hand, and new stages of relationship being marked by official declaration had been forgotten.

2000: A New Initiative

In 2000 came a new initiative. The Archbishop of Canterbury, Dr George Carey and Cardinal Cassidy, with the blessing of Pope John Paul II called together twenty-six bishops – thirteen from each Communion from areas of the world where Anglicans and Roman Catholics exist side by side in considerable numbers. The bishops came in pairs to Mississauga in Canada to review the relations on the ground where they lived, to compare that with other regions of the world, to evaluate the work of ARCIC, to re-consider the goal of Anglican–Roman Catholic relations and to ask, where do we go from here? Bishop Tony Farquhar and Bishop Sam Poyntz were the pair of bishops who travelled together from Northern Ireland.

This was an extraordinary meeting grounded in an opening time of retreat, in daily prayer and meditation, and the daily celebration of the Eucharist.[4] Never before had such a high-level group of Anglican and Roman Catholic bishops met together. At first it was clear that some of the pairs of bishops, like the pair from Ireland, knew one another well. They were used to working together and responding to the conflicts of their home situation together. Others hardly knew one another. Walking around the campus the bishops began by reflecting in pairs on the degree of life they shared at home in their own very particular situations. Then the regions exchanged stories, learning from one another about good practice and just what possibilities already existed for close co-operation in life and mission. One of the moving testimonies came from the pair from Northern Ireland. In the light of local experience, the bishops recalled the theological advances in the work of ARCIC and the official responses of the two Communions to that work. At the central point of their meeting the inspirational ecumenical theologian, Jean-Marie Tillard, explored the ARCIC vision of unity in a paper entitled, 'Our Goal: Full and Visible Communion'. Then the bishops turned their attention to the future asking, 'What next?'

The time together in that retreat house in Mississauga had revealed to them a number of things very clearly. The bishops were struck profoundly by the degree of spiritual communion already shared by Anglicans and Roman Catholics. In their time of retreat, in prayer walks, as they signed each other's foreheads in the act of re-making baptismal vows, they recognised the commonality of their liturgical inheritance. But above all in the daily Eucharistic celebrations, presided over one day by a Roman Catholic bishop, the next by an Anglican bishop, they recognised the services were almost indistinguishable. It was not only one Roman Catholic bishop who left the chapel one morning close to tears, as he wrestled with the fact that we were so close but could not receive the bread and wine together around the one table. The pain of not being able to receive together at the Eucharist was palpable. The bishops also began to understand how uneven the pattern of Anglican–Roman Catholic relations is in different parts of the world. For example, the closeness of the covenanted relationship in

Papua New Guinea seemed far ahead of the almost estranged relations in some other parts of the world.

As the bishops reviewed the work of ARCIC and the official responses to ARCIC, they were impressed by how much Anglicans and Roman Catholics already share in common faith. They became more and more determined to claim the theological convergences as a firm foundation on which to move relations forward when they returned home. It was very obvious that the bishops discovered that they actually liked one another, and that as bishops from Churches with a similar polity they had so much in common. There was a commonality in the way they understood their episcopal ministries. There was general enthusiasm to regain the Malta approach of keeping theological convergence together with convergence in life and to get back on the track of 'phased *rapprochement*'.

Their final passionate Declaration, *Communion in Mission*, conveyed a sense of excitement and urgency.[5] The bishops talked of being closer to the goal of visible unity than they had dared to think at first. Even the things that still divide Anglicans and Roman Catholics were not to be compared with all that is held in common. They called the new relationship one of 'evangelical *koinonia*'. And they recognised that as bishops they had a particular responsibility to 'guide, promote, and energise the ongoing work of the unity in our churches,' and they committed themselves wholeheartedly to this task. Their main recommendation was that a new commission should be set up – an episcopal commission – to oversee the preparation of a Joint Declaration 'to promote the reception of the ARCIC agreements, as well as facilitate the development of strategies for translating the degree of spiritual communion that has been achieved into visible and practical outcomes.' This would be 'a new stage on our journey … to full and visible unity.' They offered a short thumbnail sketch of visible unity while admitting that it is always beyond our capacities to put into words. They ended by saying, 'In our ecumenical efforts we should keep in mind that one day we will rub our eyes and be surprised by the new things that God has achieved in his Church'. Attached to their report was a detailed action plan as guidance for the future.

2004: The Windsor Report

Enthusiasm for moving Anglican–Roman Catholic relations on, it seemed, had been regained. Things began to move rapidly. IARCCUM, a bishops' commission, was set up, charged with the task of describing the life already shared between Anglicans and Roman Catholics; offering an account of the goal of the enterprise; setting out the theological agreement and convergences that already exist on the basis of the ARCIC agreed statements; while at the same time being honest about remaining differences and outlining the practical steps that could be taken by Anglicans and Roman Catholics to share together in life and mission. It seemed that Anglican–Roman Catholic relations were back on track. Theology and praxis were not now to be separated. The intention was to prepare a Common Declaration, which might be signed at the highest level of authority marking a new stage of Anglican–Roman Catholic relations, another stage in the 'phased *rapprochement*'.

The Commission worked swiftly and enthusiastically, rather like the first theological Commission had done. IARCCUM's work was near completion when it was halted by an unexpected event – the consecration of an openly gay man as a bishop in the Episcopal Church in the USA. There were those who thought it inappropriate now for any official change in relationship between the two Communions, and there were Roman Catholics who questioned what sort of Communion they were in dialogue with when Anglican provinces seemed to act so contrary to the agreements of the ARCIC statements on the exercise of authority in the Church.

Nevertheless, the bishops at Mississauga had pointed to the degree of communion that Anglicans and Roman Catholics already shared, much more than they had at first dared to imagine. When Archbishop Rowan wrote to Cardinal Walter Kasper, the head of the Pontifical Council for Promoting Christian Unity, asking the Roman Catholic Church to accompany Anglicans in their troubles, the Cardinal replied acknowledging that because of that closeness there could no longer be such a thing as unilateral action.

What happens in one Communion necessarily affects the other. At times like this we need more conversation not less. A small group of theologians, including four from IARCCUM, was given the task of reviewing what had happened in the Anglican Communion in the light of the convergences of the agreed statements of ARCIC, particularly in the area of authority and decision making. Had Anglicans acted in accordance with the developing pattern of authority in the Church as set out in these statements? The report of the group was a major input to the internal Anglican Commission set up by the Archbishop of Canterbury to respond to what had happened. That group produced *The Windsor Report*, whose recommendations included asking ECUSA (Episcopal Church in the USA) to 'express regret that the proper constraints of the bonds of affection were breached in the events surrounding the election and consecration of a bishop for the See of New Hampshire, and for the consequences that followed, and that such an expression of regret would represent the desire of the Episcopal Church (USA) to remain within the Communion.' The Episcopal Church was also invited to effect a moratorium on future consecrations of those living in an openly gay relationship.[6]

Growing Together in Unity and Mission
The Pontifical Council for Christian Unity seemed encouraged both by the work of the joint Anglican–Roman Catholic theological group and also by the response and recommendations of the Windsor Commission. As a result of this, IARCCUM was invited to complete its work. But things were not exactly as before. The document is not published as a Formal Declaration to be signed at the highest level of authority in both Churches, as was envisaged by the bishops at Mississauga. *Growing Together in Unity and Mission* is an agreed statement of the bishops who prepared it and is now for discussion in both Communions. Although the work of IARCCUM was brought to a successful conclusion, the status of its work was significantly changed.

The first part of *Growing Together in Unity and Mission* sets out what Anglicans and Roman Catholics agree in faith, harvesting the doctrinal convergences of the ARCIC conversations. At the same time it honestly records the remaining areas of difference. The second part offers a series of practical proposals for developing

Anglican–Roman Catholic relations around the world for the sake of shared service and mission. It is not possible for one international document to address the specificity of every local situation. Nevertheless, there are suggestions in the areas of sharing of faith, joint study of the faith, co-operation in ministry and shared witness in the world, which if taken seriously could move Anglican–Roman Catholic relations into a wholly new level and mark a significant step on the way to that goal of full visible communion, which was the vision that attracted the bishops at Mississauga.

Conclusion

The story of the provenance of the latest Anglican–Roman Catholic agreed statement from the episcopal group shows the importance of the search for agreement in faith – agreement that is sufficient and required to help the Churches recognise in one another the Church of Christ. It also shows how convergence in faith needs to be accompanied by convergence in life. The consensus and convergence in faith has to be embedded in the way the two communities live together sharing in worship, mission and ministry that mirrors the agreement in faith. The story also shows the importance of friendship as the seedbed in which theological dialogue and co-operation in life can blossom. This is so clearly shown in that first meeting of Archbishop Michael Ramsay and Pope Paul VI, and in meetings of Archbishops of Canterbury and Popes ever since. That same friendship was evident among the bishops who met in Mississauga and among the members of the ARCIC Commissions and of IARCCUM.

The story shows too the special responsibility for the unity of the Church that belongs to those entrusted with the ministry of oversight. *Growing Together in Unity and Mission* comes from bishops and is addressed in the first instance to bishops as leaders in mission and unity. If all the bishops of the two Communions were to share the commitment of Bishop Tony Farquhar to the unity of the Church, then the future of Anglican–Roman Catholic relations would indeed be full of promise.

Notes

1. 'The Malta Report' in Alan C. Clark and Colin Davey (eds), *Anglican–Roman Catholic Dialogue, The Work of the Preparatory Commission* (London: OUP, 1974), pp. 107–116.

2. *The Final Report of the Anglican-Roman Catholic International Commission* (London: CTS/SPCK, 1982).

3. 'The Observations of the Congregation for the Doctrine of the Faith on the Final Report of ARCIC I, 1982', in Christopher Hill and Edward Yarnold (eds), *Anglicans and Roman Catholics: the Search for Unity*, (London: CTS/SPCK, 1994).

4. The papers and reports of the meeting are published in *One in Christ*, n. 39 (2004/1).

5. Ibid.

6. *The Windsor Report 2004*, the Lambeth Commission on Communion (London: Anglican Communion Office, 2004).

PERSPECTIVES

11 Inter-Church Relations in a New Ireland

Rev. Tony Davidson

In his book *Travels with Herodotus*, the Polish journalist Ryszard Kapuściński makes the point that modern people are in danger of falling into the trap of a new kind of provincialism. He quotes T.S. Eliot:

> It is a provincialism not of space but of time; one for which history is merely the chronicle of human devices which have served their turn and been scrapped for which the world is the property solely of the living, a property in which the dead hold no shares.[1]

Kapuściński feels he is delivered from provincialism by reading the ancient historian Herodotus on his travels:

> To protect myself from this temporal provincialism I set off into Herodotus's world, the wise experienced Greek as my guide. Although Herodotus was always straightforward, kind and gentle in relation to others there was always with me the feeling of rubbing shoulders undeservedly, perhaps presumptuously but always thankfully with a giant.[2]

As Churches in Ireland travel into a new future, it is good to spend time in the company of prodigious writers from the past. In this essay, I want to look at the prophet Ezekiel; his sermons, skillfully delivered, have the ability to deliver us from a certain type of provincialism. I will look at the context of Ezekiel and some of his main themes before applying his themes to our context in Ireland.

A Context of Victimhood

Ezekiel is called to communicate with a people who comfortably sang, 'By the rivers of Babylon we sat and wept when we remembered Zion. How can we sing the songs of the LORD while in a foreign land?' (Ps 137:1) They were victims carried off to Babylon from their native Jerusalem, nostalgically missing their home city with its superb Temple. Ezekiel was born in 622 BC into a family of priests. His father was Buzi, probably a Zadokite priest based in Jerusalem. Educated as a priest in the homely environs of the Temple, the young Ezekiel's education was disrupted in 597 BC when he was caught up in an international war. Jerusalem was besieged by the Babylonians.

The Siege of Jerusalem was marked by tension, moral compromise and slaughter, from which women and children were not exempt. The psalmist brings to God his anger at unresolved conflict, expressing these harsh words, 'O Daughter of Babylon, doomed to destruction, happy is he who repays you for what you have done to us – he who seizes your infants and dashes them against the rocks' (Ps 137:8-9).

Ezekiel is called to communicate with a traumatised people; they were victims carrying with them to Babylon images of bloody destruction and cruelty. So, how does he communicate with them?

Theological Reflection – A Mobile God

Ezekiel is given a vision of God, which inspires him for his ministry. The book begins when the priest turns thirty at the river Kebar, one of the canals or tributaries of the Tigris and Euphrates. Ezekiel, like the other exiles, would have assumed that God was a static God who had an elaborate, sophisticated and intricate home in downtown Jerusalem. The assumption was that God lived in the Temple, the finest building in the city. So if Yahweh was there in Jerusalem, he could not be here in Babylon.

But the 'there' at the end of chapter 1, verse 3 does not refer to Jerusalem, but refers to this small, insignificant river in Iraq: the Kebar: 'There the hand of the Lord was upon him'.

This thought is further reinforced by the vision that God gave Ezekiel, who wrote down what he saw. He describes in some detail a desert storm coming from the north (Ezek 1:15f). In the midst of the wind and the flame are four living creatures, each of whom were multi-faced and had wings. Ezekiel adds that they each had wheels. In fact, they had wheels within wheels, which had the effect of enabling them to turn or swivel, giving them mobility and flexibility.

Ezekiel is learning that God is not restricted to Jerusalem. He is a mobile God who can move, adjust, twist and turn. Ezekiel's vision of God went on to inspire future generations of God's people to redefine their own image of God.

This mobile God is seen clearly in the gospels as the God who left heaven and came to earth in human form. This God is the Messiah who moved freely around Israel speaking, healing and showing compassion. This is the Messiah who did not stay in a grave outside the city walls but was mobile and rose from the dead, moving freely around ancient Israel, triumphant over death. After the day of Pentecost, this God pushed his people out beyond Jerusalem, into Samaria, then to the ends of the earth.

Pastoral Engagement – A Sympathetic Prophet

To speak to a people who were receiving traumatic news, Ezekiel shared in their plight. By the rivers of Babylon he made a model of Jerusalem. For three hundred and ninety days, Ezekiel acted out the siege of Jerusalem (see chapters 4 and 5). As a skilled mime artist he gathered huge crowds who watched as he acted out the latest installment of the impending crisis in the Middle East. He shared in Jerusalem's famine and its victimhood. His unshaven state was a symbol of how his home city was suffering.

The culmination of his agony comes when his wife dies. She is described as 'the delight of his eyes' (Ezek 24:16). Yet suddenly he loses the one who was closest to him. To the astonishment of his community, Ezekiel does not go through the customary bereavement practices.

Since it was well known how much they loved each other, observers wondered at his lack of emotional response. Ezekiel responds by explaining that it is a sign to the people (Ezek 24:20ff). God himself had lost the delight of his eyes – his Temple. Ezekiel's personal distress is not only linked to the people's political and spiritual distress, but also with God's own personal distress. The prophet's tough words of challenge emerge out of shared grief and agony.

Prophetic Challenge – An Alternative Agreed Story
The exiles had believed that God was on their side protecting them against any invaders. During Ezekiel's enacted siege of Jerusalem, he begins by means of signs to demonstrate an emerging alternative story. The story, as told until then, was beginning to break down. He tried to show them that God is not on Jerusalem's side. God in fact seems to be on the Babylonian side using the pagan enemy to judge Jerusalem. God chose Israel to be a light to the nations, but the people have worshipped other gods and have not even had the morals of the nations around them. He wants the exiles to start to take responsibility for their own plight (Ezek 5:7ff).

After the exile, Ezekiel's preaching becomes orthodox. The returning Jews did not return to idolatry; they interpreted the exile as judgement.

In chapters 25 to 30, the prophet has a series of sermons about how Yahweh will judge other nations. One by one the prophet lines up Ammon, Moab, Edom, Philistine, Tyre, Sidon and Egypt for judgement. Ezekiel wants to show how the children of Israel were sinned against as well as sinning; they were caught up in a complex Middle Eastern problem, to which each nation has contributed.

He also shows them that potential allies like Tyre or Egypt may be false allies. The people of Tyre were the traders of the ancient world. It may have been tempting for the exiles to look to trade to free them from their plight, but the prophet warns them of the dangers of trade freed from moral responsibility.

They may also have been tempted to rely upon the might of Egypt with its wealth and strong military. He uses the image of a reed, of which there were many along the banks of the Nile. If you leaned on the reed it snapped and you were left bruised and on your back. In the same way, if you leaned on Egypt it would snap for it was an unreliable ally. It was powerful and rich but devoid of any moral character (Ezek 29:6, 7).

Visionary Leadership – Images of Hope
Towards the end of his book, Ezekiel paints pictures of hope. The valley of dry bones comes alive as the prophet preaches and prays (Ex 37:1ff). The exiles beside the river cannot become a living community and a witness to God's truth, love, justice and righteousness again without God's Spirit. In the prophet's dream, the Spirit comes from the four winds; this is a symbol of how the Spirit comes from every corner of the earth.

Another image concerns a river whose source is in the Temple; it moves outwards through Israel bringing life and hope even to the desert. As the exiles listened to Ezekiel preaching, they were plunging into the river of life, getting caught up in God's global plan for all people from all nations. God will make them a blessing, not just for themselves, but for all the nations of the world. So the people might not just sing Psalm 137, but also Psalm 98:1: 'Sing to the LORD a new song, for he has done marvelous things; his right hand and his holy arm have worked salvation for him'.

A Context of Victimhood
I write this essay out of the experience of being in a pastoral ministry in First Armagh Presbyterian Church since 1994, as well as being involved in inter-Church work on an all-Ireland basis.

In County Armagh, many Church people in both communities are still living with horrible images of violence burnt into their collective memories. There is no agreed story of what happened during the Troubles. One community feels it was a victim of British oppression, while the other feels that it was a victim of Republican violence. Recently I attended a public hearing in Armagh organised by The Consultative Group on the Past. It was obvious that atrocities that happened to relatives or colleagues or to themselves were still fresh in their minds, even after more than thirty years. Versions of these stories are still being told to the next generation. Political developments can have the effect of leaving those who suffered most feeling even more exposed, vulnerable, angry and frustrated.

As Ezekiel helped his society to come to terms with change, so Irish Churches are called to accompany their people through this time of change in our history.

Theological Reflection – Mobile God

The challenge for us in 2008 is to still see God as a God who is not restricted to one church building in a town or one theological tradition. God is greater than our human institutions. In the reformed tradition we talk about Jesus Christ being the only King and head of the Church. As Christ is mobile enough to move around traditions, so should we as his followers be mobile enough to move around, worship, witness and learn as we watch the traces of Holy Spirit operating in different Churches in Ireland today.

This is as great a challenge to those who follow a more liberal ecumenical agenda as for those who follow a more conservative evangelical agenda. Could God have been moving, even in the most fundamentalist of Churches? Has He been changing the perspective of those who have opposed ecumenism for more than a generation, so now, on a daily basis, they can work the principles of reconciliation out in government in Stormont?

It would be rather sad if those who have been working to help understanding now adopted the self-righteous pose of the elder brother in the story of the prodigal son, and thought that God could not have been working among more politically and religiously conservative Churches. One challenge for the Irish Council of Churches and the Inter-Church Meeting will be to develop relationships creatively with these Churches in the future.

Pastoral Engagement – Sympathetic Prophets

Those of us who seek to lead Churches in new directions into the future cannot avoid the pain of past atrocities. We have to enter into the pain of people who suffered through the Troubles, sitting where they sat, feeling their tears and experiencing their emotions of anger, disillusionment and even hatred. Unless we come to terms with the reality of what was done to both sides of our community, we well not have the credibility to help people to move towards a better future.

It is noticeable how few pastors and priests who lived and worked through the Troubles are now serving in the border area or in bitterly-divided communities in Belfast and other troubled places. Most of us were not there when the most horrible atrocities occurred. Therefore, it is important for us to ask sympathetic questions and allow people to tell their stories. As Dietrich Bonhoeffer writes: 'We need to listen with the ears of God to the words of God'.[3]

Prophetic Challenge – An Alternative Agreed Story

The temptation for society is to look to economic expansion to bring hope. We are still tempted to look to free-trading Tyres and powerful Egypts for salvation. Duncan Morrow, CRC Chief Executive Officer, points out that economic expansion cannot mask sectarian divisions: 'Sectarian division in our society is pernicious cancer not a minor illness'.[4]

In a recent letter to newspapers, some ministers based in north Belfast commented how community relationships in their area had deteriorated in the past year, and how it was necessary for the Northern Ireland Executive to include community relationships in the programme for government, rather than just concentrate on economic prosperity.[5]

In a community where there are two distinctive stories, we need to work on finding a common story that will help us create a genuine future based on truth and filled with hope. In his book, *Embrace and Exclusion*, Miroslav Volf writes: 'We should seek to see things from their perspective in the hope that competing justices can become converging justices and eventually issue in agreement'.[6]

To find a common story involves prophets in all Churches challenging us all to think about the past and take responsibility for it. There is no doubt that the past is messy, muddled and complex. We minister to people who sinned and were sinned against. However, we need to ask questions about our own past. How have we contributed to the Troubles? To what extent have the Churches in Ireland been idolatrous in the sense that they have allowed the easy identification of Protestantism with unionism and Catholicism with nationalism to mutate into a situation where political, cultural and denominational identity takes precedence over Christian identity?

I suspect we all need help from people from other traditions to pose difficult questions and begin to answer those questions. I would suggest a series of small meetings in safe places where stories can be told and people listened to attentively, so that locally we receive new angles on the stories that still haunt our society.

The long search for peace has meant that no one received entirely what they had hoped for. In one sense, some 'nightmares' came to pass: Sinn Féin did not achieve their slogan 'Brits out,' instead they have helped administer the British presence in Northern Ireland. The DUP have not restored unilateral unionist rule, but must work daily with those they vowed they would not work with. Churches may be experiencing an element of God's judgement as well as his grace – perhaps the world is not listening to the Churches because the Churches together had not listened attentively enough to Jesus.

Visionary Leadership – Images of Hope

Ezekiel initially only saw a valley of dry bones, but by word and spirit he sees a vast movement of people. Looking at Co. Armagh, observers might only see the dry bones of terrorism, division, slaughter, thuggery, smuggling, criminality and despair. However, under the surface in Co. Armagh, God's Spirit is beginning to work bringing life, reconciliation, righteousness and truth. Even during the Troubles there were many examples of ordinary people doing extraordinary things in the absence of much support and encourage-ment from religious and political leaders. People attended funerals in Churches of a different tradition. They helped each other out on neighbouring farms. They played sport together. For example, in the Armagh area, golf, soccer and even rugby and GAA were all played together. In shops and businesses, people worked together without nastiness, through the most difficult and divisive of times.

Local Council officials have been working cordially together seeking the welfare of the whole city long before the Good Friday agreement was even thought about. Ordinary people created the space for politicians to become celebrity peacemakers. John Paul Lederach made this point in a lecture in November 2007 in Belfast: 'Local communities and the cross stitching of communities represent a central if not the key aspect to understanding constructive change'.

From these small tributaries of peace, a deeper river is now developing. All Churches need to get caught up in the flow of what God is doing. In the past Ireland has been regarded as a byword among the nations. People worldwide might have thought of it as a place where Christianity did not work. Now we can dare to pray that we might become a model for other nations to work out their differences together in peace.

The ancient scriptures can still deliver us from provincialism. Christian pastors need to proclaim together that Messiahs do rise from graves, and Churches do come alive. There is hope for lost sheep, for exiled minority communities and for dry, divided Churches. The Holy Spirit never allows us to lose hope; we can already sing together a new song, for the Lord has done marvellous things.

Notes

1. Kapuściński, Ryszard, *Travels with Herodotus* (London: Allen Lane, 2007), p. 271.
2. Ibid.
3. Bonhoeffer, Dietrich, *Life Together* (London: SCM Press, 1974), p. 75.
4. *CRC News,* January 2008, Vol. 7.
5. *Presbyterian Herald,* February, Edition 6.
6. Volf, Miroslav, *Embrace and Exclusion* (Nashville, TN: Abingdon Press, 1996), p. 213.

12   *Upside-Down and Outside-In*

Michael Earle

I t was a beautiful afternoon on that north Antrim coastline. The neat drills of seed potatoes in the neighbour's paddock had been carefully sown a month before. Each row bore the promise of good financial returns once the harvest was in. The birthday party had just ended, but one red balloon had escaped and was being blown across the field, chased by a small boy. Each time he tried to catch the string attached to the balloon, the wind would lift it in another direction across the field until the balloon finally disappeared from view over the hedge. Its journey, however, could be traced from the child's footprints left behind in the earth, twisting in circles, cutting right across the neatly ploughed furrows, re-arranging the distinctive soil patterns, causing future angst for both the boy's parents and the farmer next door.

In a bizarre way, might this be a glimpse into how we do church in God's fields today – in carefully managed denominational furrows that have long traditions of doing things on their own? Or by letting the Spirit flow freely through God's people in a community, bringing them into new relationships with each other and creating glimpses of another way of being church together?

We only have to think of places like the Meeting of the Waters in the Vale of Avoca to know that the most turbulence comes at the point where separate rivers meet and combine to form a new stream flowing in a new direction. That turbulent interface is the place of change and transformation; the place that carries the seeds of the past, present and future; the place where new life and energy can help sustain tired old ways, as well as a creative space where Christian Churches can celebrate and share the story of the Cross and Resurrection with a changing population in a post-modern, post-nationalist, post-Christendom context on this island.

Many are committed to develop this upside-down way of building God's Kingdom, and have faithfully kept the ecumenical flame alight during exceptionally challenging times on this island. As this baton gets passed on, it's been my privilege to serve sixteen Churches on this island as they respond to Jesus' call to be members of the Body of Christ in their witness, action and love for each other.

As Executive Secretary of the Irish Inter-Church Meeting and General Secretary of the Irish Council of Churches for the past four years, my comments are inevitably partial and time-limited. As an English-born New Zealander, I'm usually seen as the outsider on this island. However, I can draw on the experience of two earlier spells of living in Northern Ireland – as a politics student at Queen's University in the late 1960s and as Director of the Corrymeela Centre in Ballycastle for five years in the late 1980s – as well as from serving the Conference of New Zealand Churches for three years as its General Secretary.

Keys for Inter-Church Relations

In my experience, the keys for inter-Church relations are very much earthed in a process of creating spaces for different groups to meet, dialogue with each other, share their stories and build relationships of trust. In doing so, they may discover some common ground in their journey with Christ, be willing to let go something of their past, take some risks and some common actions together. But trust is like concrete powder, as I well remember Rev. Dr Eric Gallagher once explaining to a conference at Corrymeela. It is fragile and can be blown away by a single puff of air, yet when combined with certain key elements, it can firmly bind together the building blocks of any society. Trust is invisible but can never be taken for granted.

There are undoubted needs for Christians to use their gifts to work for theological ecumenism or structural ecumenism, for institutional ecumenism or grassroots ecumenism. However, my own reflection is that it is only when we meet each other at a personal level at the foot of the Cross – the level of relational ecumenism – and acknowledge our brokenness and weakness, our incompleteness without each other, that we can ever become the Easter people that Christ calls us to be.

As Rev. Dr Sam Kobia (General Secretary, World Council of Churches) pointed out during his visit to this island in 2007: 'Churches need to recognise that without each other, none of them is being fully church'. In sharing this incompleteness without 'the other', we open ourselves to embrace diversity.

Biblical diversity is sometimes expressed in terms of the different yet interconnected parts of the one Body of Christ (1 Cor 12:12) or the image of belonging to one flock with one shepherd (Jn 10:16). Rev. Roy Cooper, President of the Methodist Church in Ireland for 2007–2008, offers another image of Christian unity as a multicoloured patchwork quilt in contrast to the uniform sameness of a grey Army blanket. Whatever image fits, the reality of inter-Church work in a new Ireland inevitably involves embracing difference – but how big are we willing to let our ecumenical imagination flow?

Setting Out Anew from Kenya

A major international ecumenical initiative took place late last year in the global south. Described as an historic breakthrough, it was largely ignored by both Church and secular media on this island, but nevertheless carried seeds of new life, which might easily germinate in our local inter-Church landscape.

The November 6–9 gathering, called the Global Christian Forum, is the subject of another chapter in this book by John Radano, however, I would like to reflect on the Forum's concluding message, with regards to what it might suggest to us in Ireland.[1] It acknowledged the differences over ecclesiology, the scope of evangelism and mission. It acknowledged that prejudices had been allowed to shape understandings of different Church traditions. It went on to affirm that unity was first and foremost God's gift through the work of the Spirit, and that there was a need to be brought into relationship with one another for the sake of the witness to the gospel. By moving out of familiar ground and meeting each other on common ground, mutual love was able to flourish, dialogue grow and collective action taken to overcome divisions within the Christian family.

Mindful of the challenges and opportunities to share the gospel, pursue justice, love, mercy and walk humbly with God (Mic 6:8), Forum members made a commitment to deepen this journey, convene local/regional events and call on all those who confess God as Father, Son and Holy Spirit to work together so that all of humanity may come to know the fullness of life in Christ (Mt 28:19-20; Col 2:10).

The vision behind the Forum speaks to hearts and minds wherever we live and minister. We only have to think of the enormous diversity that lies amongst the nearly six million people who live on this island and are separated by the two political and legal jurisdictions: the numbers of new migrants from Europe, Africa and further afield; the variety of faith traditions they bring with them; the impact of the Celtic Tiger and the recent peace process on the economic, political and cultural life of our neighbours here; a local culture of conservatism with one of the highest levels of Church attendance in Europe and Church leadership that is predominantly male and clerical; and the realities of growing inequality and those feeling alienated, excluded or just ignored in this land of a hundred thousand welcomes.

The Global Forum's Challenge to how we do Inter-Church Work

The Global Christian Forum challenges our approach to how we do inter-Church work at national level on this island. There are at present two inter-Church structures that bear witness to a difficult history of theological difference. They have been created as instruments of unity and, very significantly, both have always operated on an all-island basis, crossing the legal and political jurisdictions that historically have divided this island along geopolitical lines.

The Irish Council of Churches (ICC) has a long history dating back to 1922 when it was one of the first fifteen National Councils of Churches created around the globe to address Church unity. It has grown in recent years from its pan Protestant origins and now embraces fifteen member Churches, including the historic Orthodox Churches (Antiochian, Coptic, Greek, Romanian, Russian), Anglican (Church of Ireland), Lutheran, Moravian, Reformed (Presbyterian), Methodist, Free Churches (Non-Subscribing Presbyterian, Religious Society of Friends/Quakers, Salvation Army), Evangelical House Churches (Lifelink Network of Churches) and an African Pentecostal Church (Rock of Ages Cherubim and Seraphim). Seven of these Churches have joined the Council since 1997.

The Irish Inter-Church Meeting (IICM) provides an informal forum for these fifteen member churches of ICC to meet with the Roman Catholic Church in Ireland represented by the Irish Episcopal Conference. It met for the first time in 1973 at Ballymascanlon, Co. Louth and has since met twenty-one times. A committee meets three to four times a year to keep the momentum moving forward, as well as to provide oversight of groups responsible for social issues and theological questions. One of the unique features of this structure is that everything it does is undertaken on a 50:50 basis. This is evident in its model of co-leadership, equal representation in any forum, and in its shared responsibility for finance, planning and resourcing. It brings together a total network of three thousand two hundred and fifty parishes/faith communities around the island and provides many forums for prayer, dialogue and witnessing together.[2]

The vision behind the Global Christian Forum points to the need for more chairs to be brought to the table where these Irish Churches meet. There are more than twenty Churches on this island that have not sought membership of ICC, and over forty-five independent or ethnic Churches from a Pentecostal tradition that have never, in my understanding, been invited to enter into a shared dialogue with the mainline Churches involved in ICC or IICM.

In spite of different emphases in theology and ecclesiology, we all share the Lord's Prayer with the opening words to 'Our Father,' we worship and pray to Jesus as the one Lord and Saviour, we talk about unity and communion. Yet for all kinds of historical and belief reasons we are not in relationship with each other – we do not even meet and pray together. Our common witness to Christ and to Christ's prayer 'to be one' remains fragmented, divided and lacking in credibility to an increasingly secular world.

The language of ecumenism is contentious and divisive on this island, often associated with political surrender and betrayal, yet the task given by Jesus Christ who prayed that 'all might be one' (Jn 17:21) remains in front of us all. So we must expect blessings to flow from making this commitment together and discover 'how good it is when brothers (and sisters) live together in unity' (Ps 133:1).

In a world of division, inequality, fears of global recession, addiction, greed, violence and exclusion, the ways of the gospel call the Churches to walk together and be signs of God's Kingdom; to be counter-cultural in building the common good based on peace with justice; to care for creation; to be the Salt in our communities; to stand with our brothers and sisters in need; to work together in our community's margins and darkest places; to welcome the gift of the 'other'/the stranger; and to be known for our love for each other. 'If you have love one for another, then all will know that you are my disciples' (Jn 13:35).

Extending the Patchwork Quilt of Faith and Visible Unity

So what steps need to be taken to create spaces to widen the table, draw up extra chairs and see each other as brothers and sisters in Christ? How can we extend this patchwork quilt of faith and visible unity in Christ? How can we be encouraged to move beyond the dry walls and hedgerows of separation that mark our beautiful countryside and use our imagination to see what the view of God's created land might look like from above/Heaven? How can we be encouraged to move beyond our denominational drills of seed potatoes and follow the child's footsteps in chasing the red balloon across our ecclesiological divisions?

It is only the Spirit that can encourage and guide us to seek change. But we can draw on the model and experience provided by this Global Christian Forum to move out of ground we feel comfortable and familiar with; to catch a glimpse of what could be the promise of new sacred space together on this island; to be willing to follow Jesus and enter the turbulent waters of change and transformation to become brothers and sisters in Christ in new ways.

In recent years, there have been many glimpses of new spaces created around the table and signs of communion building taking place within the Christian family on this island. Countless inter-Church projects have been undertaken at the local grassroots level, ranging from shared worship to youth and community action projects, coordinating overseas aid and emergency responses.

I'd like to highlight one example in west Belfast, which is aimed at transforming relationships between Catholic parishes and local Protestant congregations.[3] The Unity pilgrims from Clonard Monastery and local Catholic parishes quietly join congregations from other traditions in their Sunday worship. They experience a shared fellowship or communion from realising that what unites them is greater than what divides them, and share an occasional meal together. In four months last year this group planted seeds of reconciliation among thirty different congregations, seeds they believe will help build visible unity and identify in a new way what divides us. Again it is building local relationships in Christ that lie at the core of this witness.

At a broader level, it's been a privilege to see local Churches from different traditions working together in developing expressions of intercultural worship that are driven by new migrants;[4] creating opportunities to appreciate the richness of worshipping in ethnic styles very different from their own; choosing to use a single community space for their local worship in a new town; an ecumenical group inviting theologians from different traditions to wrestle with them over contentious issues like the Eucharist; the Dublin Council of Churches inviting the Catholic Archdiocese into its membership; two widely respected leaders from the Catholic and Presbyterian Churches invited to become ecumenical canons at

St Patrick's Anglican Cathedral in Dublin; ecumenical communities meeting together for the first time to build on each other's experiences; seven thousand members from different African Pentecostal Churches coming together to fill the Point (Dublin) for an all night worship celebration; the clergy in North Belfast speaking out together about the urgent need for government to address the sectarian divisions in their community and make an unambiguous commitment to a Shared Future policy.

There is much more good news to share about Churches working together in both jurisdictions, adding value to what can be done together rather than separately. This is borne out in the work undertaken by Christian Aid Ireland, the Irish School of Ecumenics, local Church forums, Churches' Community Work Alliance, Irish Inter-Church Committee on Social Issues, Eco Congregation Ireland, Parish-Based Integration Project, Faith and Order study days with staff and students from different theological colleges – to name but a few.

This is not to deny the realities of increasing secularisation, creeping congregationalism, youth disaffection and neighbourhood separation caused by twenty-five-feet-high peace walls and gated communities. But the signs of hope and innovation are there to be seen and appreciated. These are often located away from the centre, closer to the cutting edge on the margins, in spaces that are often as unpredictable as a braided New Zealand river.

Conclusion

It's an enormous privilege to be part of this inter-Church ministry on this island and at this remarkable time in its history. There are thousands of hands available to be used in the Lord's work and mission on this island. There remain countless opportunities for the Irish Churches to follow the red balloon and be led by the freedom of the Spirit in 'cross-ing' boundaries, overcoming our divisions and being mutually accountable to each other's Church and Christian Unity committees.

The experience of the recent Global Christian Forum could inspire us to extend our imagination and space at our tables to work in new, open and inclusive ways. May we build on the road we have travelled on together to strengthen our relationships, our public witness and credibility of what it means to be the Body of Christ on this island. May we have the courage to move out from ground that is now familiar, discover the breadth of God's tent in our midst and engage with new allies in presenting a gospel perspective on issues of the day that concern governments and civic society. May we continue to build the common good and work together in the dark places to break down injustice and the barriers between 'Us' and 'Them'. May we discover in this process more of what it means to be in Christ and listen to the voice of the one Shepherd.

Most importantly, as Bishop Tony commented recently at a gathering for theology students of different denominations, it is important that we come away from each ecumenical gathering we attend with joy and hope in our hearts that we have met the Lord and glimpsed something of the gift of unity that he has promised to those who follow him. Thanks be to God.

Notes
1. www.globalchristianforum.org.
2. Further details of the work undertaken by both structures can be found in the annual reports and on the website www.irishchurches.org.
3. www.clonard.com.
4. www.iccsi.ie.

13   *Ecumenism as an 'Exchange of Gifts'*

Susan Gately

2007 was a year of two important international ecumenical meetings in Europe that opened up new vistas in inter-Church dialogue, one was held in Sibiu, Romania and the other in Stuttgart, Germany. In this article I would like to reflect on some aspects of what these gatherings might say to us regarding ecumenism today. In short, Sibiu reminded us that we have to exchange our riches, while Stuttgart underlined how the gifts of each Church belong to everyone. It is good to keep before us this communion of goods, spiritual and material, in which we all share; a communion that we can all foster together as Christians.

Up until now, ecumenical relations between the Churches often attempted what has been called the method of 'convergence', that is focusing on what we have in common in order to push forward towards unity. Recently, for instance, Cardinal Walter Kasper, President of the Pontifical Council for Promoting Christian Unity, has commented on the need to discern this common faith together in a harmonious spirit:

> Only resting on the common faith is it possible to dialogue on our differences. And this must happen in a clear and non-polemical way. We must not offend the sensitivity of others or discredit them. We must not point a finger at what our ecumenical

interlocutors are not and at what they do not have. Rather, we must witness the richness and beauty of our faith in a positive and accepting way. Others expect this same attitude from us.[1]

The Cardinal also emphasised how ecumenism must be more than an 'exchange of ideas'. It is an 'exchange of gifts' from our traditions, heritage, spiritualities that can be an enriching way forward in ecumenical dialogue:

> If this happens, then between us and our interlocutors there can be, as the Encyclical *Ut Unum Sint* (1995) says, an exchange not only of ideas but of gifts that mutually enrich. Such an ecumenism of exchange is not an impoverishment, but a reciprocal enrichment. In the dialogue founded on spiritual exchange, theological dialogue will also have an essential role in the future.

However, this exchange demands a context, an atmosphere, a 'soul'. That's why 'spiritual ecumenism' is said to be the very soul of the ecumenical movement and must be promoted by us in the first place.[2] More specifically, it requires promoting a spirituality of communion:

> Without a true spirituality of communion, which permits making space for the other without renouncing one's own identity, our every effort would lead to arid and empty activism.

The Third European Ecumenical Assembly in Sibiu

The theme of an 'exchange of gifts' emerged at the Third European Ecumenical Assembly in Sibiu, Romania in 2007. The setting itself spoke of exchange. The historic city of Sibiu is one of the classic contested areas of Transylvania and a meeting place of three cultures (Romanian, Hungarian and German) and four Churches (Orthodox, Catholic, Lutheran and Reformed).

There were two thousand five hundred delegates in attendance at the Assembly, including an Irish delegation of thirty, made up of fourteen Catholics, eight Presbyterians, three members of the

Church of Ireland, two Methodists, one Romanian Orthodox, one non-subscribing Presbyterian and a representative of the Irish Council of Churches.

'The Light of Christ Shines on All' was the theme for the gathering, which had its foundation document in the *Ecumenical Charter,* which emerged out of the Second European Ecumenical Assembly in Graz in 1989, and which sets out a framework for Christians to work together in various areas.

During the six-day event in Sibiu, delegates considered common actions under the headings: Unity, Spirituality, Witness, Europe, Religions, Migration, Creation, Justice and Peace. In a huge tent erected in the business centre of the city, high-hatted Greek Orthodox clergy mingled with Anglican and Catholic bishops in their red or black cassocks. One member of the Presbyterian delegation from Northern Ireland commented that: 'It was thrilling to walk in and to see that huge gathering of Christians from so many different nations. For me it was a little foretaste of heaven'.

Gift, Dialogue, Truth
It was clear at the Assembly that the exchange of gifts passes through a 'dialogue of truth' between Churches and this can be painful. 'No church by herself can represent the whole spectrum of colours within the light; no church alone can reflect the light of Christ,' said Bishop Huber, Chairman of the Council of the Evangelical Church in Germany, lamenting the Vatican statement that had been released earlier in the summer using the expression that ecclesial communities are 'not Churches in the proper sense of the word'. One Church's claim to be the 'true manifestation of the foundation, Jesus Christ,' Bishop Huber said, inevitably downgraded other Churches and obstructed the 'common radiance and shine of the churches.' The wound of different understandings lay open for all to see.

'I know that many of my Evangelical brothers and sisters felt hurt by this statement', commented Cardinal Kasper, who received a rapturous welcome as he mounted the stage in the huge tent, 'I am not unaffected by it, either. I too had problems with it for the hurt and pain of my friends is my hurt and pain as well'. He went on, 'It was not our intention to hurt or belittle anyone. We wanted to bear witness to the truth, just as we expect other churches to, and just as other churches already do'.

However, the Cardinal also added, 'Cosy ecumenism and fake ecumenism, which are all about being nice to each other, do not get us very far. The only way forward is a dialogue of truth and clarity'. Central to the Churches' wound of disunity is the different understanding of church and the Eucharist. As a result, the lack of a common Eucharist is 'for many a heavy burden,' said Cardinal Kasper, 'but it does not help to conceal wounds. We need to leave them open, even when there is pain; only then can we treat them and, with God's help, heal them'.

Significantly, the cardinal went on to affirm how spiritual ecumenism is the heart of ecumenism, because only the gift of 'God's spirit can reconcile hearts.' Ultimately, what those who took part in Sibiu came away with were the moments of sharing and exchange with people, who met for the first time in the forums, open-air concerts, the coffee-bars and the liturgies. The group of participants returning to Ireland expressed the wish that the Sibiu meeting would not finish there. The project has only begun. The Sibiu final message provides many pointers for common exchange and action. Together with the *Carta Oecumenica,* this message puts before us another invitation to take a further step in our relationship with one another.

The Dialogue of Life: Christian Movements Share their Gifts

A particular form of recognising the gifts that God has poured out among Christians came earlier in the year, in May 2007, at another international meeting, this time in Stuttgart, Germany, and linked up via satellite to many cities around Europe. It was something of an expo of the many 'riches' contained within the Churches in the movements and communities that are coming to life across the Churches.

The meeting itself had its roots in a major event that took place at Pentecost 1998 and marked a milestone in the Catholic Church. On that occasion, many of the new ecclesial movements in the Catholic Church came together around Pope John Paul II in an occasion that was marked by an explosion of life and colour. In his address, John Paul II described the new movements as an expression of the 'charismatic' dimension of the Church, one that is 'co-essential' (along with the institutional dimension) 'to the divine constitution of the Church.'

The following year, 1999, the Catholic and Lutheran Church signed the historic Joint Declaration on Justification at Augsburg, Germany. On that very afternoon, fifty or so leaders and coordinators of movements and communities within the Lutheran tradition in Germany met up with Chiara Lubich of Focolare and Andrea Riccardi of the St Egidio Community. They recognised that the central experience of their groups and organisations, Catholic and Lutheran, had the same root. All are the work of God. And so the question arose, how can we go ahead together? 'Let's not make plans', Chiara Lubich suggested, 'God writes the music. The score is in heaven. When we meet let's seek together to listen to the Holy Spirit and to follow Him'. This 'listening' led to the first Together for Europe gathering in Stuttgart in 2004, the year ten countries acceded to the European Union. It was a journey of discovery for the many who attended, including Irish representatives of a number of communities. The movements and communities did not know each other. This was new ground.

Together for Europe 2007

However, the Together for Europe 2007 gathering was different. Between the two Stuttgart events, the journey had gone ahead. Members of different movements had visited each other, become friends, developed a heart-felt respect for the work of God, present in other communities, in other Churches. They had begun the 'exchange of gifts'. Meeting in Stuttgart, there was a palpable feeling of being part of one family. While Pope Benedict XVI toured Brazil and final frenetic preparations for the Eurovision Song contest in Finland were taking place, a little bit of Christian history was being made in Germany.

Nine thousand members of Christian movements, from all the denominations, gathered for the second Together for Europe. They represented an impressive two hundred and forty Christian movements and communities, from the Catholic, Anglican, Orthodox, Lutheran, Evangelical and even Free Church traditions. Some of the groups are well known: Charismatic Renewal, Alpha, Focolare, L'Arche, St Egidio, YMCA, but there were many more, all demonstrating the extraordinary imagination of God.

A group called 'Nativitas', for instance, was there. It was founded by a Belgian musician who was advised by a priest that she was too artistic to be a missionary! She went on to set up a series of homes in Brussels and three orchestras. She asked God to send her a husband – she didn't have time to look. He did, and together they work for the materially poor and the lonely, bringing them music and help through this 'Nativitas' community.

Another new community was a movement of mothers praying for their children (Mothers Prayers). Set up in 1995 by a mother, it is now spread to eighty-six countries with hundreds of thousands of mothers involved in thousands of prayer groups. 'Are you surprised?' I asked founder Veronica Williams: 'I am astounded. It is awesome what the Holy Spirit is doing'.

In his message at Stuttgart, Cardinal Kasper commented that 'The movements keep the Church young'. The Church is not only an old institution with a long tradition, 'but she must always become young, and the movements help.' In the Hanns-Martin-Schleyer-Halle on Saturday, 12 May, the atmosphere was electric. Nine thousand people were there in person and one hundred thousand more followed the event in fifteen languages via the internet and satellite television. In fifty-two European cities, parallel meetings took place. One was in Belfast.

Movements and Communities in Ireland

These movements and communities exist also in Ireland. Indeed, the Together for Europe gathering was marked also in Belfast just four days after the historic event of the new power-sharing assembly. It seemed like a miracle. The Together for Europe meeting had been planned for some nine months, initially through the co-operation of Charis and Focolare and then too with others. It had helped to form a 'network of points of interaction' as David Stevens, leader of Corrymeela put it.

But the results of the day went beyond everyone's expectations. Over one hundred participants from movements and communities such as Corrymeela, Cornerstone, l'Arche, Cursillo, Focolare, Koinonia, Charis and Restoration Ministry and representing seven Churches, spent a remarkable day together in the Church of the Resurrection, Elmwood Avenue, Belfast, speaking 'a new language', as one veteran in inter-Church relations put it.

Not only did they link up live via satellite with the events taking place in Stuttgart, but they too had the opportunity to worship together (lead by Corrymeela and Charis) and to get to know each other's movement, each a window into the gospel and a gift for healing of wounds in the surrounding society.

Young people from Youth Initiatives and Youth with a Mission provided an upbeat injection of youthful enthusiasm into the day. Particularly moving was the l'Arche contribution as the co-ordinator Maria Garvey, together with other companions, shared the gift of their charism with everyone: 'God made all things good … There is no such thing as disabilities … We have all been created in the image of God … no one is a mistake'.

The words of the Founder of Focolare, Chiara Lubich, relayed from Stuttgart also resonated, as she invited participants to recognise the face of Jesus forsaken, who cries out 'Why?' in every division, darkness and trial.

'Today has been an answer to our prayers for many years', said one participant at the Belfast meeting. 'This moment of unity with other movements has come in God's time – days after the opening of our Government Assembly. The patience and love of many people has borne fruit'. Afterwards, Maria Garvey from l'Arche wrote: 'It is the seed for a community of communities and you can't imagine how exciting I find that'.

In Maynooth, Co. Kildare, another parallel meeting brought together one hundred and fifty people for the transmission, including sixty members of an umbrella organisation for Catholic movements and communities called Tine. Rob Clarke from Youth with a Mission said he was impressed that the unity between them was built around Christ crucified: 'In other words, we are not called to some sort of cheap form of "peace love and happiness" but rather something much deeper than that'. There was recognition that it is 'because of what Christ has done that we can have this unity.'

Messages from Stuttgart and Sibiu

A 'yes' to life in all its forms issued from the two events. This 'yes' was not a nice aspiration, but a reality. At Stuttgart different groups showcased the work they were actually doing in fulfilment of that 'yes' in a variety of fields: the YMCA working with the homeless and drug addicts; St Egidio brokering peace deals in the Ivory Coast and Burkino Faso; The Teams of Our Lady and other groups supporting marriages; ten million people doing Alpha courses to experience or deepen a relationship with Jesus; the Focolare's Economy of Communion setting up over seven hundred businesses that share profits with the poor.

Uniting together to speak with one voice on issues relating to life was advocated. Denis Wrigley, Methodist and founder of Maranatha, for instance, leads a healing ministry based on the words 'Unity, Renewal and Healing', with about ten thousand members in the UK. 'The problem is,' he commented, 'that in the last few years in Britain, we haven't been doing that, and so the politicians have ignored us'. He continued: 'Western culture has turned its back on God. The secular humanistic experiment has failed. The evidence of that is in smashed families and spiralling rates of addiction, abortion and so on. We've sewn the wind and we're reaping the whirlwind. But I firmly believe if we pray as one people, and if we act together, there will be miracles'.

The Ecumenical Assembly in Sibiu, four months after Stuttgart, also relayed a positive message to the world. The delegates named ten concrete recommendations for action in areas like migration, the continued quest for Christian unity, human rights, globalisation, fair trade and climate change. Admittedly, it was difficult to achieve consensus on specific life and ethics issues. The phrase in the final message reads: 'We consider that every human being is created in the image and likeness of God (Gen 1:27) and deserves the same degree of respect and love, despite differences of belief, culture, age, gender, or ethnic origin'.[3]

143

Brotherhood Remains the Basis for Ecumenism

In his message to the meeting at Sibiu, Pope Benedict XVI said ecumenical efforts must be directed by the dialogue of truth and an encounter in brotherhood. This brotherhood grows through an increased communion or exchange of ideas and treasures. 'By now, the churches don't hide behind unmotivated courtesies,' Bishop Huber, Chairman of the Council of the Evangelical Church in Germany, explained, 'and they are able to face the challenges with clarity. At the same time, we also stress the fact that what we have in common is far more important than what divides us. We also say that listening to the Spirit we will find the way toward full and visible unity in diversity.' Cardinal Kasper echoed his words: 'We are working in a lab for the future of our churches. I think it's clear to everyone how Bishop Huber, Metropolitan Kirill and myself feel we are brothers'.

But true brotherhood will always be a dynamic open to others. Andrea Riccardi, founder of St Egidio, challenged Christians at both Sibiu and Stuttgart to be the new prophets of Europe, and as a united continent, to reach out to our poorest neighbour – Africa. In his address at Stuttgart he said: 'A united Europe is also a Europe that does not separate from its little ones, from weak and unborn life, from its old people and from its poor. We must look at these weak faces with love. This is for us not only something we must ask but something we must live day after day'.

'But how can we be happy, when our neighbours suffer?' he continued, 'And our neighbour is Africa, the great Sub-Saharan Africa … The Africa of wars, of 30 million people with HIV (out of 42 million in the world), the Africa where two-thirds are excluded from wealth'.

The call to brotherhood in faith and action was very strong: 'I take home with me, the personal encounters. Now the different churches are not just names, but people,' said Dr David Stevens. Bishop Anthony Farquar said: 'There is a temptation for people to feel they have to be apologetic for what they believe in order to be ecumenical, but I felt the Spirit of the meeting was that people felt secure to say what they believed without threatening or being threatened. We are enriched by others, and we are in a position to enrich them as well'.

Notes

1. Address at the opening of the Pope Benedict XVI's meeting with the College of Cardinals on Ecumenical Dialogue (November 23, 2007).

2. Vatican II Decree on Ecumenism, *Unitatis Redintegratio,* n. 8 and Pope John Paul II's encyclical letter on commitment to ecumenism, *Ut Unum Sint* (1995) n. 21–27.

3. The full text of the final message can be accessed on http://www.eea3.org.

14   *Practical Ecumenism*

Bishop Crispian Hollis

Three Models for Building Society

I have long been an admirer of the writings of Sir Jonathan Sacks, the Chief Rabbi of the United Hebrew Congregations of Britain and the Commonwealth. He always writes persuasively of the issues of the time and almost always from a perspective that is deeply Biblical. His latest book, *The Home We Build Together,* is no exception. In this critique of modern British society and analysis of the shortcomings of multiculturalism as a way of organising our common life, the Chief Rabbi writes:

> Multiculturalism has run its course and it is time to move on … it has not led to integration, but to segregation. It has allowed groups to live separately, with no incentive to integrate and every incentive not to. It was intended to promote tolerance. Instead the result has been, in countries where it has been tried, societies more abrasive, fractured and intolerant than they once were.[1]

In chapter two of his book he basically offers three models for the building of society and they are as follows: society as a country house, as a hotel or as a home we build together.

In the first example, there is a dominant culture in which the 'outsider' can only be a guest, albeit an honoured guest. The guest is welcome but the host always calls the tune.

In the second example – the hotel – there is no dominant culture. All are guests and all live in separate rooms, between which there are no built-in communications. Meetings between the residents are haphazard and unplanned. This is multiculturalism and there is nobody who really belongs to or 'owns' the hotel.

The third example is quite different because it involves all those who come together in a common purpose and a common activity, namely the building of a community that reflects and respects all the gifts of the participants and all that they have to contribute. The result is a community which has shared values and gifts. It is a society in which all can participate and which, to use a modern jargon phrase, all can own.

I offer this very brief summary of the thesis being proposed by the Chief Rabbi because I think it says something powerful to us – *mutatis mutandis* – about the ways in which ecumenical dialogue has developed over the years that I have been a priest and a bishop, namely since 1965.

Opening to Dialogue – Out of the Prison of the 'I'
Let me take you back to the years when I was an undergraduate at Oxford – the 1950s. At that time, Catholics really wanted very little to do with other Christian denominations, nor were they encouraged to do so. From our perspective, Catholics were right and all the others were wrong. If there was to be any development towards Christian Unity, then it could only be on Catholic terms and through a process of conversion to the Catholic Church. Young Catholics at that time did not question this, nor did they really want to. We were a self-sufficient Church; we had everything we needed and, indeed, we believed that we had an exclusive hold on truth. If Catholics were to be involved in any ecumenical work at that time, then we were truly operating on the so-called 'country house model'. We were a dominant culture, self-sufficient and self-contained, and others could only either join us or remain as guests – on the outside.

The teaching of the Second Vatican Council and especially the decree on Ecumenism, *Unitatis Redintegratio,* was to change this attitude most profoundly. In a very serious way, the Catholic Church became open – at last, some might say – to all the gifts and movements of the Spirit in all Christian people. This has led, over the years, to an increasing openness in dialogue, in worship and in common life. Increasingly Christians are comfortable with the sharing of riches and the exchange of gifts, seeing their source as being the work of the Spirit within individuals and communities.

There are very many unilateral and multilateral dialogues going on between the Churches today and all of them, in different ways, are bearing fruit. Sometimes the pace is not as swift as participants and observers would like; sometimes the response from local congregations is less enthusiastic than might be wished for. There are frustrations and setbacks which can sometimes seem to be catastrophic and destructive, but when looked at in the perspective of ecclesiastical history since the Reformation, progress since the promulgation of *Unitatis Redintegratio* has been little short of miraculous and palpably the work of the Spirit. What is, perhaps, equally important is the understanding on all sides that there can be no going back to the *status ante.* Increasingly, Christians of all traditions are realising that they are no longer living in separate rooms without connecting doors – the hotel model of society – but that they are more and more living in situations that demand the common prayer, the sharing of the riches of the different traditions and that discernment of the work of the Spirit in the hearts of all who are the followers of Christ.

The imperative to evangelise and to live and spread the Good News is more urgent than ever in our world, which seems to be becoming increasingly secular and faithless as each day passes. The proclamation – and the attainment – of redemption, as Pope Benedict XVI describes it in his latest encyclical, *Spe Salvi,* 'appears as the re-establishment of unity, in which we come together once more in a union that begins to take shape in the world community of believers … This real life, towards which we try to reach out again and again, is linked to a lived union with "a people", and, for each individual, it can only be attained within this "we". It presupposes that we escape from the prison of our "I", because, only in the openness of this universal subject, does our gaze open out to the source of joy, to love itself – to God'.[2]

IARCCUM

As far as Britain and Ireland are concerned, a major process of dialogue has been between the Anglican Communion and the Catholic Church. The work of ARCIC and, more recently, that of IARCCUM (International Anglican–Roman Catholic Commission for Unity and Mission), has been rooted in the principles of listening with an openness to what others have to say, seeking to get behind the slogans and banners of centuries of bitterness, violence and hatred in order that the truths of the gospels, enshrined in different traditions, can be discerned, valued and respected.

Bishop Tony Farquhar and I have been privileged to be participants in the International Anglican–Roman Catholic Commission for Unity and Mission. I am sure that he will not mind my saying that neither of us were invited to be part of the Catholic team, if I can put it that way, because we are great theologians. That is certainly not the case, but we are pastors and we do have a wide range of pastoral experiences, which have an important part to play when it comes to putting together practical and faithful propositions for our people. We are both deeply convinced that a unified Christian voice brings immense power and strength to the wellbeing of the home we build together. Such a home or society without the dimension of religion can only provide a very poor reflection of what it means for us to be made in the image and likeness of God. A society built without God is a society that is at the mercy of all the forces of the 'I' and 'me'. These are destructive and selfish forces, which only help us to serve ourselves with very little understanding that there is anything in human history and civilisation which can be described as 'the common good'.

South of England – Belfast

When it comes to practical, on the ground ecumenism, Bishop Tony and I work in very different circumstances. My situation is the south of England which is, by and large, tolerant and easy going.

I have grown up with Anglican roots – both my grandfathers were Anglican clergy and one of them, whose episcopal ring I now possess and wear, was the Anglican Bishop of Taunton. Both my parents became Catholics; my father before he married and my mother some years later. By the time we, the children, came along, we were a Catholic family, though my brothers and my sister and I all inherited in our genes a respect and a love for the traditions, music and liturgy of the Church of England. Many of my parents' friends were either Anglican or converts to Catholicism. In those 'prehistoric' days, practical ecumenism was alive and well in the Hollis household.

My Roman seminary training immersed me in the Roman tradition and in the Catholic faith which is absolutely central to everything I am and do, but I have always had that sense of sympathy and a certain understanding of what it means to be Anglican. My work has always involved me actively in ecumenical relationships, whether it be in the parish, the University Chaplaincy in Oxford, in my years in the Religious Broadcasting Department of the BBC or as a parish priest and a bishop. Our diocese of Portsmouth relates to three Anglican dioceses and I find myself on extremely good terms with all my fellow Church leaders, be they Anglican, Free Church or Salvation Army. We work well together and our only real regret is that we all find it difficult to persuade our congregations of the vital ecclesial and evangelical importance of working for Christian Unity. By comparison with the situation in the North of Ireland, my ecumenical furrow is a relatively easy one to plough.

Belfast and the North of Ireland, to my outsider's eye, represents an entirely different kettle of fish, and I have always felt that my Catholic brothers and sisters in the North are having to or have had to grasp with an ecumenical imperative which was really and truly a matter of life and death, both for the Province and for the participating Churches. Such has been the power and violence of sectarianism and such has been the history of bitterness and hatred that relationships between the Churches have been fraught with immense challenge and even physical danger. That has been real ecumenism, red in tooth and claw.

The Bishops in the North have been challenged hugely by the situation and I can only stand in admiration at what has been achieved. I truly believe that much of what is now established in the society of the North as the way of peace has been due to the courageous example and endeavour of the Church leaders. Bishop Tony Farquhar has been, in many ways, an ecumenical spokesman and he has brought immense personal and theological skills to the situation. To be taken around Belfast and some of its trouble spots by Tony is to be taken on a journey through and beyond the sectarian divisions. He seems to know everyone and is well received by all, no matter what their faith standing may be.

Bishop Tony would, of course, deny all this but I know, from impeccable sources, how influential he has been. There is no one to whom he will not talk, there is no one he is afraid to approach, whatever the background and circumstances may be. He is fearless but immensely loving as a human being among fellow human beings. It may well not be through talking politics or theology at all that he has been influential – more than likely, it will be through sharing his passion for football and, in particular, for Dundee United. He makes relationships, and ecumenism and peace making are all about relationships. All the theology and beautiful spirituality in the world will cut very little ice if not deeply rooted in relationships. Ecumenical relationships need courage because, in the end, they have to be relationships that express love, respect and value of the other person, from wherever they may come.

I believe that this is the major contribution that Bishop Tony has been making over the last twenty-five years and, indeed, throughout his priesthood, be it in parish or university chaplaincy. He reaches out to others; he is interested in them and he believes, with his deeply Catholic heart, that he has something of immense value to offer to and share with his many friends, and to the whole situation that has been the tragic history of Northern Ireland in our days. Through his ministry, and that of his fellow bishops in the North, the Catholic Christian voice has been heard loud and clear, whether in formal religious dialogue, in prayer and preaching, or in immense pastoral care for suffering communities.

These are some of the reasons why I find such inspiration in the ecumenical work of Bishop Tony and many others in the North today. Catholics have learned not to treat others simply as guests, who always have to toe the Catholic party line lest they remain permanent outsiders. We are not inviting guests into our Catholic country house, however tempting a prospect that may be.

At the same time, we are not becoming so 'multicultural' that it doesn't matter what anyone believes – truth in such a situation becomes relative and merely a matter of opinion. That would be the hotel in which all are guests, all have separate rooms with keys and in which there are very few connecting corridors; just shared, faceless and neutral facilities.

Bringing about the Kingdom of God

If the answers to society's problems lie in people recognising each other's gifts, pooling their energies, working together for something greater than any one single contribution, then this has to be the seed of the good life and the common good. I also firmly believe that it is part of the wonderful, Christ-given task that we have of bringing about the Kingdom of God, which is a kingdom of justice, love and peace. To work in this way throughout the community is to work ecumenically; it is true evangelisation because it is the proclaiming of God's love for the whole human family. 'How beautiful on the mountains are the feet of the messenger announcing peace, of the messenger of good news who proclaims salvation and says to Zion, "Your God is king"' (Isa 52:7).

Bishop Tony and I have been involved, as I have said above, in one of the more recent dialogues between the Roman Catholic Church and the Anglican Communion. *Growing Together in Mission and Unity* represents the fruit of the labours of IARCCUM, a Commission to which we were both privileged to belong. Its purpose was 'to offer practical suggestions on the way in which Anglican and Roman Catholic Ecumenical participation can be appropriately fostered and carried forward.'[3]

In the document, we acknowledge 'that the faith we hold in common is given us by God ... we have become increasingly aware of how increased interaction has led to greater mutual understanding, and at the same time, how this greater awareness of the extent of our shared faith has set us free to witness together more effectively ... We give glory to God, "whose power, working in us, can do infinitely more than we can ask or imagine; glory be to him from generation to generation in the Church and in Christ Jesus, for ever and ever. Amen (Eph 3:20-21)"'.[4]

The work of ecumenical dialogue and relationships is at the heart of the life of the Church and can never be regarded simply as the preserve of the enthusiasts – the so-called 'ecumaniacs'. 'The invocation "*ut unum sint*" is, at one and the same time, a binding imperative, the strength that sustains us, and a salutary rebuke for our slowness and our closed-heartedness. It is on Jesus' prayer and not on our own strength that we base the hope that even within history we shall be able to reach full and visible communion with all Christians.'[5]

I believe that not only is ecumenical work and the consequent relationships of dialogue and understanding at the heart of the Church's mission, it is crucial for the peaceful and positive building together of our common home – the society in which we live, the human family of nations and faiths.

Notes

1. Sacks, Jonathan, *The Home We Build Together: Recreating Society* (London: Continuum, 2007) p. 1.
2. See Pope Benedict XVI, Encyclical Letter on Christian Hope, *Spe Salvi*, n. 14.
3. IARCCUM, *Growing Together in Unity and Mission: Building on 40 years of Anglican–Roman Catholic Dialogue* (London, SPCK, 2007), Preface.
4. Ibid., n. 93–95.
5. Pope John Paul II, *Novo Millennio Ineunte*, n. 48.

Bringing Martin Luther and Thérèse of Lisieux into Conversation

Rev. Prof. Tom Norris

> My protectors in heaven, my favourites,
> are those who stole it, such as the Holy
> Innocents and the Good Thief. The great
> saints have won it by their works: for
> myself, I wish to imitate the thieves, to
> take it by a trick, a trick of love that will
> give me entry, me and other poor sinners.[1]

In his encyclical on ecumenism, *Ut Unum Sint*, Pope John Paul II observes that dialogue is not an exchange of ideas principally. Rather it is 'an exchange of gifts'.[2] This represents a fresh and exciting stage in ecumenical methodology. Whereas the typical method followed in the decades since Vatican II was that of seeking out convergences in areas of faith and order, facilitated by the partners speaking their respective faiths in an atmosphere of respectful listening, the new method consists more in making a gift of one's own faith and faith-life to the other. By nature the earlier method of convergences tended towards finding the lowest common denominator. A good instance of this method of convergence may be read in the Lutheran–Catholic agreement on justification.[3] A further instance of the method in operation may be seen in the documents of the Anglican–Roman Catholic International Commission.[4]

The new method of 'the exchange of gifts' underlines mutuality in the respectful offering of the particular faith-experience of one's own Church or ecclesial communion. This mutuality makes it a method that is congenial to dialogue. That dialogue is an essential way for the Churches in our time, indeed for the very future of Christianity. I should like to illustrate this truth by means of a dialogue between the founding father of Lutheranism, Martin Luther (1484–1546), and a very 'Catholic' saint and doctor of the Catholic Church, Thérèse of Lisieux (1873–1897).

These dialogue partners are very unlikely to say the least. As respectively the 'Father of the Reformation' and a typical instance of the Catholic ethos, Martin Luther and Thérèse of Lisieux live in different times and places and communities. Religiously, culturally and historically they appear to inhabit different planets. The division of Lutherans and Catholics has been both institutionalised and historically hardened, at least until quite recently. It seems that any possible 'exchange of gifts' is simply out of the question between two persons who are so distant and different from one another. Could they become partners in dialogue? Could they personify the new methodology of the 'exchange of gifts'? Have they in fact gifts to offer one another? This article sets out to address these questions.

The Experience of the Human Condition

Both Luther[5] and Thérèse[6] aim at the demolition of one's own ideal of perfection to make room for God's perfection in the creature. The concrete circumstances leading them to this discovery, however, were quite different. Unfortunately, these circumstances have tended to dominate our historical imagination and to marginalise the core of their actual discoveries. If instead one turns to history, it is possible to read the flow of late Medieval Theology as the emergence of a new clarity with regard to the theology of redemption, and specifically the notion of justification. That notion deals with what divine revelation has to say to us on how we cease being the enemies of God, outside his Kingdom and life, and actually become his friends. How do we access salvation? This query is the key to Luther, for whom everything begins with the questions, 'How can I find a merciful God?' and, 'How can I become certain of his mercy?'

These questions arose from the deep experience Luther made and wrote about as early as 1518. It was the experience of tribulation upon the vivid realisation of his own sinfulness *(Anfechtung)*.[7] Recent careful research has shown, contrary to popular Catholic historiography, that Luther's discovery is rooted in St Paul's teaching, 'I do not do the good I want, but the evil I do not want is what I do' (Rom 7:19): 'He didn't mean, as is often thought he meant, that it's impossible for us to avoid doing wrong. Our problem is much more intimate and rather complex'.[8] Even when we do what is good there is generally the tendency to do it for our own good, and not out of disinterested love. In a word, we are afflicted by a certain curvature, a turning back on ourselves that hides under the most noble deeds and motives. This is the real drama, since none of us can free ourselves from this 'curvature'.

When people notice this they realise they are not able to love God as they ought – with their whole heart. They are a failure with regard to the basic commandments of God. It is clear that to attempt, by one's own unaided efforts, to climb out of this pit is both perfect Pelagianism and utter folly. It is this experience of his radical inability to obey the first of all the commandments that causes Luther's *Anfechtung*.

Thérèse made the *same discovery,* though of course in entirely different personal and historical circumstances. She realised very well her incapacity to reach the heights of holiness. This came home to her in the well-known episode of the elevator in Paris that fired her imagination.[9] The intuition of there being a lift that takes one straight to the God and Father of our Lord Jesus Christ strongly encouraged her to 'seek out a means of getting to heaven by a little way, a way that is straight, very short and totally new,' as she wrote. A scholar remarks that 'her battle is to wipe out the hard core of Pharisaism that persists in the midst of Christianity; that human will-to-power disguised in the mantle of religion that drives one to assert one's own greatness instead of acknowledging that God alone is great.'[10] Another authority remarks: 'With the utmost severity Thérèse directs her attack against every ascetical practice that aims, not at God, but at one's own perfection, which is nothing more than a spiritual beauty treatment'.[11]

The Discovery of God: Eternal and Merciful Love!

The realisation that *God is eternal merciful Love* plays out an organising role for both Thérèse and Luther. When Luther realises his lack of love, his total inability to love God and neighbour as they ought to be loved, with all the tribulation that this caused him, he makes a second discovery – God bends down towards our human weakness and misery and recreates us: 'He does this on one condition: that we believe, that is, that we abandon ourselves to him with complete trust. This is Luther's great and liberating discovery'.[12] Luther says it like this in his famous Heidelberg Disputation of April 26, 1518: 'God's love does not find in the world what he loves, but he creates it'.[13] That's what makes God's love different from human love: human love is attracted by what is lovable, God's love loves the unlovable and makes the unlovable lovable! In his remarkable commentary on the *Magnificat*, written in 1521, Luther sums up his own experience of God: 'God looks upon those, who, like Mary, live in the consciousness of their own nothingness, and fills them with his gifts. He smites and rejects those who are full of themselves and consider themselves just'.[14]

Thérèse made a remarkably similar discovery with important implications. She read in the Scriptures, 'Whoever is a little one, let him come to me' (Prov 9:4). Thérèse learns that 'progress does not come through acquisitions but through losing everything; it does not mean climbing, it means descending.'[15] She searched further in the Scriptures and found the text, which brought joy to her soul: 'As one whom the mother caresses, so will I comfort you: you shall be carried at the breasts and upon the knee they shall caress you' (Isa 66:12-13). One begins to notice her particular penchant for *sola scriptura!*

Here she saw the 'Little Way' begin to peep out. It consisted in the reality of the love of God made visible in his incarnate Son

(Rom 8:39) and bending down to us. He who described himself as 'the Way' (Jn 14:6) was suddenly discovered by Thérèse as the actual fulfilment of the powerful intuition that had come over her in Paris. Yes, a Way that was 'very straight, very short, and totally new'! One did not have to climb. Less still did one 'need to grow up, but rather one had to remain little and become this more and more.' One *enters as if into an elevator.*[16] To do so, however, requires that one has the heart of a child in order to trust totally in the eternal merciful love of Christ and his eternal Father. To a novice who laments her own lack of spirituality she says: 'I see that you have taken the wrong road; you will never arrive at the end of your journey. You are wanting to climb a great mountain, and the good God is making you descend it; he is waiting for you at the bottom in the fertile valley of humility'.[17] She wants to walk 'in the way of childhood.'[18] Here one meets with Thérèse's principle of *sola gratia.*

The Word of the Cross

Famously, Luther discovered and underlined the centrality of the Word of God for the Christian life. Its importance lay in the fact that it 'was through his word that God made us alive, generated us, nourished us and educated us.'[19] At the core of this word, however, there is 'the word of the cross.'[20] On the Cross the Word of God is finally revealed and unpacked in a manner that is as incomparable as it is wonderful. In Christ, God went down to the deepest abysses of human life. Luther perceives this kenotic descent of the Son most vividly in the cry of forsakenness of Jesus on the cross. Why this cry? he asks. He replies, along with Isaiah and St Paul, that Jesus has so made all that is ours his own, as to become 'accursed' (Gal 3:13) and even 'sin' for us (2 Cor 5:21), and to experience all its consequences. He writes, 'And this is the superabundant mystery of divine grace towards sinners, namely, that through a wondrous exchange, our sins are no longer ours, but Christ's, and the justice of Christ not his but ours. The truth is that he has stripped *(exinanivit)* himself of his justice so that we might be clothed and enriched by it, and that he has taken on our sins in order to liberate us from them *(exinaniret)*'.[21] In this way he has become 'our wisdom, and our virtue, and our holiness, and our freedom,' as St Paul stresses in his *First Letter to the Corinthians* (1:30). In other words, 'Jesus communicated to us, as in a true espousal, his justice – that is to say, "he justifies us."'[22]

Thérèse for her part is fascinated by the tremendous mystery of the *kenosis* of Jesus for sinners. This is the inspiration of her early entry to Carmel and, more particularly, of her self-offering to the love of God that has been poured into our hearts by the Holy Spirit (Rom 5:5). This love is revealed to us in Christ through whom we receive the grace of 'knowing the love that is beyond all knowing' (Eph 3:19). This is the love that reverses the fall. Now, 'taken in the abstract, the notion of a fall is inseparable from that of defeat and disgrace. But the same is not true in the realm of love, where a man's fall is incorporated into the law of Christ's fall, which is itself one moment in the downward movement of Christ from the Father to the world, to the Cross, to hell. For this is the realm where God or his angels quickly set everything right'.[23]

With her exceptional love for the Word of God, Thérèse saw in Jesus crucified for sinners (Isa 53:5; Rom 4:25; Gal 3:13; I Pet 2:24) the unsurpassable icon of God as Love. The Word nourished her continually, inspiring her desire to love and then fuelling that desire to love still more. The instance of her turning to *First Corinthians* in search of the light as to what mattered most in her vocation is justly famous. She discovered how to be love in the heart of the Church, her Mother. In being such love, she would live all the vocations at once, since each is, in the final analysis, an expression of love for Crucified Love: 'To be nothing else than love, deep down in the heart of Mother Church; that's to be everything at once'.[24] It is this Love that drives all vocations. It is after all the Heart of the Church as the Body of Christ.

Justification by Works or by Faith?

There is a fourth major point of exchange and convergence between Luther and Thérèse. Both *reject the Old Testament notion of justification by works*. Luther for his part explains this by means of his Christology or, more specifically, theology of redemption. His insight is synthesised in the famous principle, *simul justus et peccator,* both just and sinner. It is a point which has led to the greatest incomprehension, as if Luther wished to say, as Catholics have often insisted, that God does not truly transform human nature. However, 'Luther wanted to remind us that there's only one way of being truly a Christian and that is by continual conversion. The formula refers to the continual passing over from living according to the flesh to living according to the spirit, the passage from the old man, concentrating on himself, to the new man, completely oriented towards God and his neighbour'.[25] Only God is capable of refounding our lives, of directing them in the right direction.

Faith in this perspective means to cling to God alone, not first and foremost to our deeds or to our works. Luther does not pretend that this will be easy. The gift of such faith is God's greatest to us. That faith is his grace, and we receive it by faith alone. This does not mean that we have to remain eternally inactive or that good deeds do not have their place. There is nothing more hard working than faith! But the right order must be preserved. What is first needed, Luther says, with an image from Scripture (Mt 7:17-20), is that the tree should become good, and this occurs through grace alone. But then this tree has to bear fruit corresponding to this grace, that is to say, to produce good works.

In his 1520 treatise, *The Freedom of a Christian,* he describes a Christian as 'a free lord, above all things, and subject to none,' but also 'a servant available for everything and subject to all.'[26] Rooted in Christ, the Christian has to become in his turn 'a Christ' for his neighbour. Or, as he puts it in his *Second Commentary on the Psalms:* 'Just as Christ came from God, and has attracted us to himself, without looking for anything for himself during his life, but [only] for what would be good for us, so we too, once we have entered faith, should go out and attract others too, without seeking anything other than to save many along with ourselves through the service of all'.[27] This, then, is Christian existence for Luther: to be in Christ – faith. And, in virtue of Christ, to be another Christ – love.

Now when we come to Thérèse we are struck by something amazingly similar. She roundly repudiates what von Balthasar calls 'reckoning'. She makes her point in the most vivid terms, 'There is one science that God does not know – arithmetic'.[28] Thérèse eliminates all reckoning to make room for grace. This is her *sola gratia*. This grace is not magical but creative. And in an illustration that would surely have generated a *frisson* in her conversation with Martin, she says: 'The principal plenary indulgence, and one that everyone may obtain without the customary conditions, is the indulgence of *charity that covers a multitude of sins* [Prov. 10:12]'.[29]

It is important to say that Thérèse does not sit in judgement on anyone's labours or works, 'but the one thing she cannot abide is that human beings should boast of their works in the face of God.'[30] This calls forth the famous image of the empty hands, 'After earth's exile, I hope to go and enjoy you in the fatherland, but I do not want to lay up merits for heaven. I want to work for your *love alone* ... In the evening of this life, I shall appear before you with empty hands, for I do not ask you, Lord, to count my works. All our justice is blemished in your eyes. I wish, then, to be clothed in your own *justice* and to receive from your *love* the eternal possession of *yourself*'.[31] This text is quoted in the *Catechism of the Catholic Church* in its delicate section on *Grace and Justification*.[32]

Conclusion

These, then, are a few of the points that emerge when we imagine 'the Father of the Reformation' and the one Pope Pius XI called 'the greatest (Catholic) saint of modern times' in an exchange of faith-experiences. This article has adhered to their very words, attempting to set in motion a conversation between them, a conversation leading to the exchange of their gifts. Luther and Thérèse are two representative personages. In fact, so representative of their respective communions are they that their personal conversation becomes an ecclesial conversation. The outcome of that conversation provides fresh impetus for further ecumenical dialogue between Catholics and Lutherans. With her 'explicitly doctrinal mission ... to light up certain aspects of revelation afresh for the benefit of contemporary Christendom,'[33] Thérèse's theological audacity is reason to hope that the remaining difficulties on the road to unity of faith between Lutherans and Catholics are far from insurmountable.

Notes

1. De Lisieux, Sainte Thérèse, *Histoire d'une âme,* Lisieux, 1923, in Balthasar, Hans Urs von, *Two Sisters in The Spirit: Thérèse of Lisieux and Elizabeth of The Trinity* (San Francisco: Ignatius Press, 1998). p. 263.

2. Pope John Paul II, *Ut Unum Sint,* 1995, p. 28.

3. See Pontifical Council for Promoting Christian Unity, Information Service, n. 98 (1998/3), pp. 81–100. For an analysis of the text, see Avery Dulles, 'Two Languages of Salvation: The Lutheran–Catholic Joint Declaration' in *First Things,* Vol. 98, December, 1999, pp. 25–30.

4. For example, *ARCIC I: The Final Report* (London: CTS/ SPCK, 1982).

5. For Luther, see the work of Hubertus Blaumeiser, *Martin Luthers Kreuzestheologie* (Paderborn: Bonifatius, 1995), which breaks new ground through the careful textual examination of his writings.

6. For Thérèse de Lisieux, see Hans Urs von Balthasar, *Two Sisters in the Spirit* (San Francisco: Ignatius Press, 1992).

7. *D. Martin Luthers Werke, Kritische Gesamtausgabe,* Weimar 1883f., abbreviated as WA; for here, see WA, I, 557f.

8. Blaumeiser, Hubertus, 'Martin Luther and the Heart of the Christian Faith' in *Being One 6* (1997), p. 17; see also this author's 'Dal cuore della rivelazione al centro della vita. Dimensioni di fondo della teologia di Martin Lutero' in *Nuova Umanità XXI* (1993/3–4) pp. 387–403.

9. De Lisieux, Thérèse, *Story of a Soul* (ICS: Washington DC, 1981), pp. 207–208.

10. Von Balthasar, Hans Urs, *Two Sisters,* p. 241.

11. Görres, I.F. *The Hidden Face: A Study of St Thérèse of Lisieux* (New York: Pantheon, 1959), p. 332.

12. Blaumeiser, 'Martin Luther and the Heart of the Christian Faith', in *Martin Luthers Kreuzesthologie* p. 17.

13. Ibid., p. 18; see WA 1, 365, 9–10; WA 7, 547, 8–16.

14. Ibid., p. 18.

15. Von Balthasar, *Two Sisters,* p. 245.

16. See *Story of a Soul,* pp. 207–208.

17. Görres, *The Hidden Face,* p. 338.
18. Thérèse de Lisieux, *Histoire d'une âme,* p. 231.
19. WA 5, pp. 405, 477–478.
20. Ibid., 5, 657, pp. 27–28; see I Cor 1:18.
21. WA 5, 608, pp. 6–9.
22. Blaumeiser, 'Martin Luther', p. 18.
23. Hans Urs von Balthasar, *Two Sisters,* p. 280.
24. Thérèse, *Story of a Soul,* as quoted in *The Divine Office* III (Dublin: Talbot, 1974), p. 305.
25. Blaumeiser, 'Martin Luther', p. 21.
26. Luther, WA 7, p. 21.
27. Ibid., 5, 408, pp. 10-13.
28. Thérèse, *Histoire d'une âme,* p. 280.
29. Ibid., p. 288. My emphasis.
30. Von Balthasar, ibid.
31. *Story of a Soul,* p. 277; see *Novissima Verba* (Lisieux: Office Central), p. 37. My emphasis.
32. *Catechism of the Catholic Church* (Dublin: Veritas, 1994), p. 2011.
33. Von Balthasar, *Two Sisters,* p. 233.

16 A Brief Overview of Quaker Relief and Peace-Making in Ireland

David Poole

Recalling a Visit to Palestine and Israel

In October 1991, a delegation from the Churches in Ireland visited Palestine and Israel, with a particular concern to make contact with the indigenous Christians in those countries. A proportion of that delegation had in 1987 also been members of an Irish Churches delegation that visited the Soviet Union. Participation in such delegations inevitably opens the members to great personal contact. The opportunities to forge deep friendships and to become aware of the personal strengths – and even the weaknesses – of their fellow delegates. Bishop Tony Farquhar and I were members of both of those delegations and were thus able to renew and deepen personal friendship that has remained undiminished over the subsequent years.

In Jerusalem in 1991, our delegation went on a supportive visit one afternoon to the weekly silent demonstrations by the Women in Black – an organisation of Jewish women opposed to the Israeli occupation of the Palestinian lands. I can still recall so clearly the look of surprise, linked to a response of joy, on the face of the woman who found herself confronted by three friends – a Roman Catholic bishop from Belfast (Bishop Tony), a Presbyterian minister from Lisburn (Rev. Dr Gordon Gray) and a Dublin Quaker. I think the symbolism of the unmistakable friendship in the relationship exhibited by the three of us was of encouragement and support to that demonstrating woman, with whose cause we could so genuinely identify.

On the flight travelling back to Ireland we were treated to the inevitable long haul programme of entertainment films, particularly cartoons. At some stage I received a note, passed around the cabin from its writer, suggesting that Irish Quakers should mount a campaign against the violence portrayed in the *Tom and Jerry* films – signed Tony. It was of course mainly written and sent in jest, but inherent in the fun as usual with Tony was a serious thread of understanding and meaning. Did he really think either that Irish Quakers would mount such a campaign, or if they did would anyone take any notice of it? Perhaps he did, and perhaps we should have taken it more seriously than just a passing jest.

Quakers in Ireland

Bishop Tony would of course have been aware of the Quaker testimony for peace and non-violence, with its particular relevance to the three-hundred-and-fifty-year history of the Religious Society of Friends in Ireland. For long periods of that time-span it would have been a quiet and low-key concern – perhaps obvious to the close observer of the lives and business methods of individual Quakers or of Quaker families. However, from time to time the public might have been made more aware of that aspect of Quaker belief by the collective actions of groups of Friends or of Quaker meetings. For instance, in the 1790s when the inevitability of what became the 1798 uprising was becoming clear, Quaker meetings throughout Ireland issued advice to their members that they should dispose of all personal firearms, lest they should be taken and used against their fellow men. This direction was almost universally accepted and many Quakers broke or destroyed fowling guns or similar arms publicly. Perhaps as a result of this and their refusal to side with either the government or the rebels, although it was not an intended outcome, no Quaker (with one possible exception) died during that period of civil unrest and fighting, although many did suffer personal loss of property.

During the twentieth century, many individual Friends were active in national peace movements and anti-war campaigns. While their actions were particularly aimed at forming public opinion and influencing political actions, in most cases the removal or alleviation of the root cause of violence would also have been involved – for instance, the well known efforts of the Friends Central Relief Committee during the famine years of 1845 and 1846. In the equivalent of current value, some €21 million was distributed during that period, money given by Irish, British and American sources, mainly, but by no means exclusively, from Quaker donors.

Quaker Principles

That relief programme was characterised by a series of working criteria; principles that were new but which subsequently have formed the basis for many modern relief programmes. These included on-the-ground research of the need, the local conditions and the possible impact of donated relief, the use of non-Quaker local partners (in many cases local clergy, both Roman Catholic and Protestant) and, perhaps best known, an avoidance of any condition of belief or behaviour and no commitment for any return of the gift. Coupled with the distribution of money and materials, many groups of Quakers were directly involved in setting up and running soup kitchens in many urban centres. One of the valuable donations in kind came from the Darby Quaker family foundry in England of a supply of fifty-six iron soup boilers specifically made for this purpose.[1]

Reference has already been made to the characteristic Quaker principles that poverty and hunger, discrimination and disenfranchisement must be addressed as fundamentals of peacemaking. Internationally, British and Irish Friends mounted relief programmes in many parts of the world: Russia, post-war Europe, Africa, India and China.

Programmes such as these often underpin and give substance and credence to politically-based efforts of peacemaking, which otherwise might be brushed aside. It was significant that the 1947 Nobel Peace Prize – awarded jointly to the American Friends Service Committee and the Friends Service Council (involving

British and Irish Friends) – was specifically for relief work with post-war refugees.

In 1927, British and Irish Friends drew together several existing Quaker relief and missionary committees to form the Friends Service Council. Over the ensuing decades, FSC created a worldwide programme addressing relief needs, promoting peace and attempting to do God's will in alleviating suffering. In the opening words of 'A Testimony for Peace', published in a review of Quaker work over the century 1868 to 1968 entitled *The Past is Prologue*,[2] the basis of Quaker work is identified:

> Quaker relief work springs directly from the Society's peace testimony, from compassion towards the victims or war – war which Friends have over three centuries maintained to be contrary to the spirit and teaching of Christ. We utterly deny all outward wars and strife and fighting with outward weapons for any end or under any pretence whatever. These words came from 'a declaration from the harmless and innocent people of God called Quakers, given to Charles ll on 21st January 1661 … Within 20 years Robert Barclay (1648 to 1690) of Ury has seen the need also for Friends to carry their witness for peace into the political and international world where statesmen make decisions'.

These examples of Quaker relief and peacemaking are part of our history. In Ireland, Friends today express their practical relief programmes largely through the organisation Irish Quaker Faith in Action, which was formed in the early 1990s.

Northern Ireland
I would like at this point to concentrate further on those more recent events which fall within the personal memory and experience of both Bishop Tony and of this writer. The situation in Northern Ireland – both political and social – was a cause of great concern to many. During the 1950s and 1960s it was clear that in many ways life was unstable and politically insupportable. Quakers, particularly those living in Northern Ireland, were concerned at this situation.

Denis P. Barritt, a Belfast Quaker, who for seventeen years was the secretary of the Belfast Council of Social Welfare, Bryson House, was Chairman of the Fellowship of Reconciliation in Northern Ireland, Co-Chairman of PACE (Protestant and Catholic Encounter) and the author of a number of books addressing this concern. In 1962 he was co-author with Charles F. Carter of *The Northern Ireland Problem,* and in 1969 co-authored with Arthur Booth of the Northern Friends Peace Board in Britain the book *Orange and Green,* which was rewritten as a second edition in 1972. In 1982 he wrote *Northern Ireland – a Problem to Every Solution,* explicitly published as 'a contribution to the discussion of the future of Northern Ireland'.

Writings such as these helped to clarify and explain the political and social situation in the province. They pointed to possible ways forward which could have been peacefully pursued but unfortunately were overtaken by more radical and violent approaches. Eventually, the occurrence of serious rioting and civil unrest, including the burning of whole streets with many homes destroyed, led to internment without trial. Quakers, along with many other Churches, opened Meeting Houses as temporary shelters for those who had to leave their homes.

The Meeting House in Frederick Street, Belfast was one of these – an area of particular unrest. The resulting relationship with local residents continued after they had returned to their homes. This led to Quakers, possibly uniquely, also being concerned about the conditions endured by the relatives visiting those who had been interned in the temporary internment camp in Long Kesh. A temporary canteen was provided in accommodation erected in the car park. As the prison became the more permanent Maze prison, so too the Quaker organisation provided expanded services in a more permanent visitor centre; not just cups of tea but also a crèche and counselling services and a go-between with prisoners and prison authorities. To organise all this the Ulster Quaker Service Committee was appointed, along with a programme for children and family holidays. Later, visitor facilities were organised for those with relatives in Maghaberry prison. Looking back over the early days of these efforts, one Quaker commentator has written: 'There is much to admire, some lessons to learn, a few regrets and, with hindsight, some wry smiles'.[3]

In a separate venture by the same committee, Quaker Cottage was acquired on the slopes of Black Mountain overlooking Belfast and close to some of the city's most deprived areas. This was developed into a cross-community child activity centre, a programme that included many family-based activities. The buildings were rebuilt in 1991: 'A new white building shines out on the hillside in the morning sunshine and, as one helper once said, from there you cannot tell which of the streets of Belfast are orange or which green'.[4]

Parallel with these practical relief programmes, all of which originated from the desire of Ulster Friends in 1969 'to investigate means of relief, rehabilitation and reconciliation in our community,'[5] British and Irish Friends cooperated in their attempts to address the political impasse. During the 1970s a 'Watching Committee' was appointed with a very open brief. It was partly to plan and partly to coordinate any efforts being made by individual Friends or groups of Quakers. It was a period in which many academics and others with international experience felt that they could create a formula which would be the basis of or lead to a settlement. Later in that decade, after the Watching Committee had been laid down, the 'Northern Ireland Committee' was set up – again equally representative of British Friends and Irish Friends – north and south. A house in University Avenue Belfast was purchased as a home for Quaker representatives and as a venue for meetings. Many of these were confidential and unrecorded. Much of the impetus for the work came from the encouragement of non-Friends, who felt that Quakers had the trust and the experience being even-handed, confidential and non-involved.

The Quaker House programme was facilitated by a series of Quaker resident couples who, with the support and assistance of the members of the Northern Ireland Committee, offered a neutral and quiet venue for political and community leaders to meet. Obviously this was during a period when such meetings across religious and political divides were not possible publicly and considerable care and discretion was essential. Also on the programme of that committee and of the Quaker representatives were efforts to address, or challenge, such matters as police or Army behaviour, the conditions in prisons, the use of plastic baton rounds and similar topics. Meetings were held with people in public leadership and the Secretaries of State to discuss many issues.

All of this was well before the Good Friday Agreement and the later progress and agreements leading to the setting up of the Stormont Executive of 2007. So, how much effect can we say it had? In common with many other efforts from groups such as Corrymeela Community, PACE (Protestant and Catholic Encounters), the Commission for Justice and Peace and the Irish Council of Churches, to pick just a few, none achieved any particularly significant breakthrough, but all laid down stepping stones that led to an eventual political solution, a solution that now needs to be even more fully recognised, welcomed and cherished by those who live under its influence.

During this period, under the guidance and with the support of the Home Mission Committee of Ulster Friends, an annual young people's camp has been held at Moyallon near Portadown. Martin K. Mail has written, 'Moyallon Camp occupies an important place in the Christian life of Northern Ireland. Since the 1930s thousands of young people have had their lives affected by summer days at Moyallon when their faith was kindled or renewed. While it has been a Quaker-led event, its contribution and influence have been much wider, to the mutual benefit of the whole community'.[6]

Over the years, the camp used the Moyallon Meeting House premises, but by 2000 the accomodation was no longer suitable to hold the campers safely. A Moyallon Camp Development Committee took this matter in hand and in 2006 a newly-built residential conference centre with sleeping accommodation for about sixty people was opened. It is not only facilitating the Moyallon Camp but is available to those who wish to use it for inter-Church and social uses, and thus makes a valuable contribution in the field of reconciliation.

Recent Developments and Events in Dublin

Two hundred years ago, Quakers in Dublin set up Bloomfield Hospital, a place for Friends with disorders of the mind – an early example of sympathetic care of those with mental problems. Soon it also became a haven for non-Quakers and it developed a Nursing Home with sheltered accommodation for elderly people. In the 1980s the old medical Supervisors' House (Swanbrook House) was deemed unsuitable for this use and replaced, but found a new role as an Administrative Headquarters for the Religious Society of Friends in Ireland.

In this century, a major development was embarked upon in which the Bloomfield Hospital transferred to a newly-built facility on the slopes of the Dublin Mountains above Rathfarnham. Integral with this move was the provision of a new Quaker headquarters in place of Swanbrook House, opened in the presence of the President of Ireland, Mary McAleese, in 2006 – a building that challenges and facilitates Irish Friends, but which is also available as a non-residential conference centre or meeting venue for those who can usefully avail of the premises. It complements the residential facilities provided in Moyallon.

It is an interesting coincidence that in the same year the Ulster Quaker Service Committee became 'Quaker Service' and the Bloomfield Hospital became the Bloomfield Care Centre Ltd., both bodies incorporating as companies limited by guarantee, all, it is hoped, part of the ongoing efforts of Irish Quakers to continue service with peacemaking.

In 2007, Irish Friends hosted the Friends World Committee for Consultation triennial meeting, held in King's Hospital, Dublin in August. This was the seventieth birthday of the FWCC – the organisation that connects Friends throughout the world. In Dublin, over three hundred Quakers gathered from forty-one countries – bringing together the rich and very varied tapestry that is Quakerism worldwide – of which Irish Friends are a part and a reflection.

Conclusion

In this essay to honour Bishop Tony Farquhar, I have concentrated on the contribution of Irish Quakers in the complementary areas of relief services and peacemaking. The Yearly Meeting of the Society of Ireland, in its membership of the Irish Council of Churches since its foundation in 1922, has repeatedly emphasised its commitment to the process of inter-Church relations in Ireland.

Tony's note, all of twenty years ago, poking gentle fun at Quakers' attitudes to violence as portrayed in *Tom and Jerry* cartoons may indeed have been prophetic. I hope he would have supported a current Quaker campaign which seeks to raise awareness of the extent to which violent death and violence generally are being used, without questioning, as entertainment on television, video and film.

The campaign, initiated by Ballitore Friends, which seeks to question that use of violence and killing, is asking TV stations not to show any violent deaths for entertainment purposes on just one day each year. The date chosen is 2 October, the date of Ghandi's birthday, which is the United Nations World Day of Non-Violence. The Irish Inter-Church Committee on Social Issues has recently decided to fully support this Quaker initiative, a position supported by the Irish Inter-Church Committee.

Notes

1. Goodbody, Rob, *A Suitable Channel* (Bray: Pale Publishing, 1995).
2. Friends Service Council, *The Past is Prologue 1868 to 1968* (FSC: London, 1968).
3. Neil, Joyce, *A Brief History of the Ulster Quaker Service Committee,* unpublished monograph, 1998.
4. Ibid.
5. Ibid.
6. Chapman, Arthur G., *Moyallon Camp Fellowship: A Record of God's Grace 1934 to 2001,* Home Mission Commission of Ulster Quarterly Meeting, 2001.

17 *Journey Towards Shalom*

Bishop Samuel Poyntz

D r Martin Luther King once declared he had a dream that justice would roll down like waters and righteousness like a mighty stream. But there are a number of steps to be taken on the journey to Shalom which will include the processes of reconciliation and justice.

Too often the *crie de coeur* of a Northerner challenged to forgive the seemingly unforgivable has been heard: 'How can I forgive when no one will admit that they have done wrong?'

Such a question is not seeking the instant answer as we try to grapple with endemic violence and hatred, nor is the questioner dodging the obligation to forgive ignoring hurts, fears and bitterness. Such a superficial approach can only lay itself open to the charge of Jeremiah, 'They dress the wound of my people as though it were not serious. "Peace, peace," they say when there is no peace' (8:11).

Forgiveness

Forgiveness seems to be at a premium nowadays. Arabs cannot forgive Jews, Serbs cannot forgive Bosnians, Hutus cannot forgive Tutsis. What about forgiveness in our own land?

Consider what the New Testament has to say concerning God's forgiveness of us and our forgiveness of others: 'Forgive us the wrong we have done as we have forgiven those who have wronged us'. This is the only petition in the Lord's Prayer which is immediately followed by the terrifying words, 'If you do forgive others the wrongs they have done, your Heavenly Father will also forgive you: but if you do not forgive others, *the wrongs you have done will not be forgiven by your Father*'.[1] The same principle runs right through the New Testament as when St Paul writes to the Colossians, 'Forgive one another as the Lord forgives you' (3:13).

Forgiveness cannot be dismissed as costless and painless, as in the snide phrase of the philosopher Heinrich Heine, 'God will forgive me, that's His business'. There can be no forgiveness without justice. Justice must be done and be seen to be done. Above all, Christian people should know the cost of forgiveness. Almighty God did not close an eye on sin and evil. On the Cross God's judgement and grace are supremely revealed.

Thus an individual who has come to know the forgiveness of God through Christ may feel it necessary to hand himself over to the judicial authority, to pay his debt to society for the crime he has committed. True forgiveness requires honestly facing the fact that wrong has been done, without any excuse and acknowledging it for what it is. The Belfast-born C.S. Lewis put it this way:

> Real forgiveness means looking steadily at the sin, the sin that is left over, after all allowances have been made, and seeing it in all its horror, dirt, meanness and malice and nevertheless, being wholly reconciled with the man who has done it.[2]

It is perhaps those who have been forgiven most through the blood of Christ who can find it in their hearts to forgive in this way. Think what hate does to the person who hates. What the unforgiving spirit does to the person who cannot forgive! This comes home on reading some words of Corrie Ten Boom, who suffered much in World War II. She wrote:

> Since the end of the war I had had a home in Holland for victims of Nazi brutality. Those who were able to forgive their former enemies were able to return to the outside world and

rebuild their lives, no matter what the physical scars. Those who nursed their bitterness remained invalids. It was as simple and as horrible as that.

If someone does not acknowledge the wrong they have done, forgiveness can be offered but no true reconciliation will take place. In July 1996, Michael McGoldrick courageously stood by the grave of his son, murdered by so-called loyalists in Portadown, and said, 'I forgive you' but that offer was not taken up. Those who perpetrated the terrible deed had not the courage to admit their guilt. The same went for the late Senator Gordon Wilson – again there was no repentant to receive the forgiveness he offered and so lead to true reconciliation.

One way of being able to forgive those who have done evil or whom we deem as enemies is by talking to them face to face, or by costly and generous action. Jomo Kenyatta was a terrorist who became the first President of Independent Kenya. On taking office, he broadcast to the nation. In the course of his remarks, he said to the white people, 'You have done terrible things to me personally and to the black people of this country. I want to tell you today that I forgive you and wish to set all this in the past'. He went on to say, 'We, black people, have done terrible things to you, can you in your hearts find it possible to forgive us?'

Forgiveness involves more than penitential words. God does not say to humankind, 'I forgive you'. The Word has to become flesh. God was in Christ reconciling the world to Himself (2 Cor 5:19). In so many reconciliation situations, words will be needed but without deeds they will not be believed. Usually it takes a deed to undo a deed. Gestures and actions speak louder than words.

The magnitude of the wounds and wrongs in Ireland require more than words for the reality of forgiveness and reconciliation to be realised. Acts of reparation and restitution need to take place and this leads to the question of what can be done corporately to facilitate this process. The Churches – even divided as we are – can become communities of forgiveness, modelling the honesty of facing the truth of the past by making public confession where there has been wrong done.

When Archbishop Robert Runcie of Canterbury visited Dublin, he asked the forgiveness of the Irish people for all the evils done by his people in this land over the centuries. Cardinal Daly, in a similar vein, preaching during the Week of Prayer for Christian Unity 1995 in Canterbury Cathedral, asked the people of Britain to forgive the people of Ireland for the evils they have perpetrated in the past. Archbishop Eames in an address commemorating the Irish famine, while acknowledging that some forty members of Church of Ireland clerical families had sacrificed their lives in tending victims, said: 'We seek the forgiveness of God for the failure to meet that disaster in ways which would have reduced unbelievable suffering – we seek the forgiveness of each other for the past'. Some years ago, two small groups of Presbyterians and Roman Catholics in Belfast quite independently asked each other's forgiveness for the wrongs done over the centuries. All this is commendable, but is a further step required?

The Irish Inter-Church Meeting Committee might consider drafting confessions to be accepted at the highest level by all the 'mainline Churches' on this island. This could be ratified at roughly the same time by the Roman Catholic Hierarchy, the General Synod of the Church of Ireland, the Presbyterian General Assembly, the Methodist Conference and so on. The draft would be difficult to draw up but if the right words were found the statement could prove to be of historic significance, ranking alongside the post-World War II Stuttgart German Church Statement and the Kairos South African Prophetic Call. There is much in all our past histories of which we should be ashamed; events which have left a legacy of hurt, stress and bitterness. To name but one among many on the Church of Ireland side, at the highest level we never raised an official voice against the Penal Laws which had such a savage effect on Roman Catholics and Presbyterians. On the Roman Catholic side, mention might be made of the way Church of Ireland membership has been decimated through the rigorous imposition of the 1908 *Ne Temere* Decree until more recent legislation, but the legacy lingers on. Scratch the surface, and we find all have hurts.

Equally, political leaders can make symbolic acts to express the penitence of the people. For example, Willi Brandt knelt at the memorial to the Jewish Warsaw Ghetto. In South Africa the dismantling of the structures of Apartheid acted as a symbol of repentance allowing space for forgiveness to be offered. We do well to heed the prophetic words of Alexander Solzhenitsyn, the great Russian writer and Nobel Prize Winner, whose Christian faith was formed in the crucible of suffering in a Siberian Labour Camp. He wrote:

> I can only discover one healthy course for everyone living, for nations, societies, human organisations and above all else the Churches. We must confess our sins and errors (our own, not those of others), repent and use self-restraint in our future development.

We need to be aware of the plank in our own eye before contemplating the speck in our brother's eye. Forgiveness is the only thing that can break the vicious cycle of revenge and prevent the future being determined by the past:

> History despite its wrenching pain
> Cannot be unlived but if faced
> With courage need not be lived again (Maya Angelou).

Behind reconciliation there lies a number of steps: sorrow, confession, repentance, reparation, forgiveness. One does not go directly from A to Z. One moves by steps, A to B, B to C, C to D and so on, involving a process. Sometimes steps are taken forward; at other times there may be a step backward. Reconciliation is always creative, bringing into being a totally new situation.

Justice
Another step in this journey is required: if one is to experience Shalom, there can be no forgiveness without justice. How often have we heard victims on both sides of the Northern political divide calling for justice? Frequently in their minds they will be thinking of terms of 'retributive justice'. However, justice is a many-sided concept and there are a variety of approaches among these; 'restorative justice' is a pearl of great price.

177

The idea of restorative justice (R.J.) has been highlighted by Dr Howard Zehr, Professor of Justice of the Eastern Mennonite University, Virginia. For him and many others, R.J. is not a soft option and where vigorously pursued can lead to offenders not re-offending again. He wrote in *Changing Lenses* that R.J. can be linked with the Old Testament (Biblical) notion of Shalom (Peace). He maintains that over the years he has come to realise just how distorted our western world understandings of justice are. So much can be traced back to street justice based on the idea of 'tit for tat'. If some person does wrong to another, then the offender must suffer in return and this attitude permeates our institutional schemes of justice.

R.J. has been used all over the world in more recent times. At a Dublin lecture last year given by Dr Heather Stacey, an Australian Professor, a concept was backed whereby the offender and the victim meet face to face in the presence of family and friends of both, assisted by trained facilitators and the good will of the courts, police and so on. Everyone can contribute to the discussion on the damage done, how it can be repaired and how to ensure it will not happen again.

R.J. has been tried and not found wanting. For example, men like the Chief Constable of Thames Valley, Sir Charles Pollard, backed this method a decade ago. Take this Canadian example: a young man killed his two friends in a drink-driving accident. Instead of a prison sentence, which frequently is the norm, the parents of the deceased boy suggested, with the approval of the courts, that this young man must visit schools in the province recounting the story of what it is like to kill one's two best friends and the legacy of drink-driving. This proved a powerful deterrent, resulting in a domestic decline in drink-driving cases in subsequent years. Nearer home, the Annual Report of Restorative Services for 2006 tells of a service through Tallaght District Court, while only a few months ago the prison chaplains in the Republic of Ireland in their report for 2006/2007 stated that 'The prison system is a finishing school for the advancement of criminality, especially where the service is overcrowded and dysfunctional'. The Chaplains supported R.J. as an alternative to be considered by the courts.

This idea needs to be vigorously pursed by the members of the judiciary and parliamentarians, Church leaders and the media, who can contribute so much to shaping public opinion. It could make a real contribution to the healing of our unseemly political/religious divides, but also to those who come before the courts for all sorts of crimes. To quote again Dr Martin Luther King, 'There is a fierce urgency of the Now'.

Punishment must punish and it must not be removed from the equation that leads to Shalom any more than the other steps: sorrow, confession, repentance, reparation, forgiveness, justice. The emphasis must not only be on the restoration of the offender, but also of the victim. Here is a system not to be conducted by kangaroo courts – republican or loyalist – but by governments, judges, police and probation facilitators.

Not Bound by Hoops of Steel
In 1974, Dr Isaac Cohen, then Chief Rabbi of Ireland, said: 'A culture that is content to remember the tragic history of their forefathers and is bereft of any ambition to evolve a new life out of reasonable opportunities for the fullest expression of personal expression is a culture that is bound by hoops of steel, which certainly hold fast whatever they contain, but forbid the possibility of living growth and development'.

Gestures and actions will always be important in confidence-building measures. A fruitful way forward might have been a Truth and Revelation Commission, similar to that in South Africa and elsewhere, but this was a step too far for some when first mooted. Yet it is likely that some sort of independent Truth Commission dealing with the past will some day be a required essential element, if there is to be healing of the psychological wounds and divisions. The Lord Eames/Denis Bradley Consultative Group on the Past is charged with seeking a way forward and will have to give due attention to this and other factors in the future. As a community, we have come a long way since the signing of the Good Friday Agreement in 1998, which has led to the restored devolution of power in the Northern Ireland Assembly. The almost unthinkable has happened with the various political parties in the North, including the extremes of the Democratic Unionist Party and Sinn Fein sharing power, much to the chagrin of fundamentalist groupings, religious and political, which tend to look for total victory and find it hard to compromise.

Quite unexpectedly, the Berlin Wall came tumbling down and the South African Apartheid system collapsed. Our walls of bitterness and hatred, hurts and fears do not reach to heaven. One day these too will disappear. In the years to come, 2007 could mark a defining period in the totality of our relationships on the island of Ireland. Either we bring our shared Christian insights to bear on seemingly intransient problems or we return to violence, which spells ultimately disaster and defeat.

Finally, we need to keep before us the aspirations to Shalom, that peace which passes all understanding because it is grounded in the hospitality of God, who in Christ draws the whole creation into one – a peace which reconfigures difference – where diversity is cherished and we accept that Almighty God reaches out to both offender and offended. Opportunities are turned into complementary facets of a multi-faceted revealed Truth. This is the Truth and we must bear witness to it if we are to experience Shalom.

Notes

1. My emphasis.
2. Lewis, C.S., *Essay on Forgiveness* (New York: Macmillan Publishing Compay Inc., 1960).

18 The Servant as Subversive: Secular Literature and the Christian Tradition

Prof. Eda Sagarra

Anyone who wants to become great among you must be your servant (Mk 10:43).

A particular source of hope for the future of the Christian Church today is its renewed emphasis on service and the centrality of the figure of Christ the Servant. Service takes many forms, not least the readiness to put oneself and one's experience of ministry, as Bishop Tony Farquhar has done, at the service of Christian unity. The present article explores in the Bible and secular texts, features of the ancient literary topos of the master as servant and the servant as master.

Secular literature in the western world has shown a far greater consistency in its presentation of those who serve than those who command. Servant types, as first elaborated on the Greek and Roman stages, have varied little in essence over the centuries. From the time of Aristophanes to Cervantes, from Plautus and Terence to Molière, Goethe and Brecht, the servant figure has proved an extraordinarily enduring feature of the European literary imagination. At one level, the literary servant has a purely functional role, present to entertain, to serve the exposition and to promote the action; at another level he – less often she – becomes the vehicle to challenge received certainties, to subvert cherished values but also to convey deeper truths.

Common to the ancient classics and to western literature up to the age of Enlightenment is the notion of the hierarchy of literary genre, as mirroring the 'natural' or 'God-given' hierarchical structure of society. Baroque artists liked to render the latter in terms of a social pyramid, with (depending on one's affiliation) the Pope in tiara or the crowned Holy Roman Emperor at its apex and the various 'orders' ranged in seemly pattern beneath. Renaissance and baroque poets – the latter so concerned with 'policing' and containing – produced the theoretical underpinning for literary composition.

The distinctive literary genres of epic, drama and poetry and their sub-divisions, such as tragedy and comedy or, in the case of poetry, the sonnet, the ode, the song, the epigramme, were seen to have a correspondence or equivalence in the various social echelons. The sonnet celebrated noble men and women and addressed lofty themes; a song was for 'mere' burghers – or carefree youth. The Silesian-born Martin Opitz (1597–1638) ordained in his influential *Book of German Poetry* (1624), that while tragedy had as its subject kings and heads of states, the proper domain of the servant (as of the student and the peasant) was comedy. The servant was of his nature a figure of fun. His assignment to the comic mode derived from a notion of preordained and distinctive categories of 'stock', of mental and moral capacity determined by birth and 'blood'. As in latter-day racial theories, this was seen as immutable. However, from the perspective of the age, it was not viewed as burdensome, since the servant was regarded as incapable of self-reflection.[1] When the servant figure begins to reflect, as in Lessing, Diderot, Goethe, and Mozart's *Figaro*, western literature has reached the modern age.

Servant Types

Traditionally the servant is 'foolish', ergo comic, because he is governed solely by instinct and drives. The master comes to know right conduct by education and the use of reason, whereas the servant, like the ass, only reacts to physical stimuli. Aristophanes provides an early example in the figure of Xantias, slave of the god Dionysus in *The Frogs*. He appears on the stage seated on his master's ass, filling the air with his laments at the weight of the luggage, suspended over his shoulder from a large fork. Like the ass, he is a beast of burden, but a stubborn one, who must be treated accordingly. In Mozart's *Magic Flute* (1791), Tamino must undergo a series of trials, which he does not understand but willingly accepts, in order to purify himself and become 'a man'. The loose-mouthed Papageno has to submit – under vigorously expressed protest – to a variety of punishments to curb his drives, including wearing a padlock on his mouth. While Tamino is persuaded by moral argument, and the growth of consciousness plays a vital role in leading him to make the appropriate moral choices, Papageno in learning to control his carnal appetites for food, drink and women, is governed by his fear of the stick. And yet the servant, as Cervantes' immortal Sancho Pansa or Goldoni's Truffaldino in *The Servant of Two Masters* (1743) demonstrate, can also stand for common sense. The world 'below stairs', as the realm of servants came to be called, provided a rich training in knowledge of human nature. If the master 'above stairs' were to behave in a manner unseemly to one in authority with the duty of care, he would forfeit respect. No man is a hero to his valet, runs the old adage. The butler of the Lord Curzon, later Viceroy of India, put it equally crisply. To a house guest, angered at his host's gratuitous rudeness, his 'man' is said to have observed, 'but of course Lord Curzon is not a gentleman'.

Roman comedy created three distinctive servant types which still endure, both in text and image: the clever servant *(servus callidus)*, the slow-witted *(servus frugi)* and the messenger *(servus currus)*. Examples of the first include Mercury[2] in Plautus' *Amphitryon*, Molière's Scapin *(Les fourberies de Scapin)*, or in our own day the incomparable Sir Humphrey in the television series, *Yes, Minister*.[3] Sancho Pansa or the Fool in *King Lear* belong to the second category. The third, as we shall see, proves the most fertile of all, embracing an astonishing variety of human types and categories, from the herald to the notion of metaphor as mediating the 'message' of a text,[4] and including a host of divine and satanic emissaries. While comic servants down to the eighteenth century until the emergence of the soubrette are almost exclusively male, one enduring female servant can trace her origins back to Homer. This is the old nurse Eurykleia in the *Odyssey*. She combines in her person the idea of memory linking past and present (as an old servant), closeness to nature/the natural order of things (as a woman) and the ideal of service as self-surrender. In the last aspect, she could be said to anticipate the servant in Christian literature and indeed service as the Christian ideal. As she touches his skin,[5] it is she, and only she, who recognises the returning Ulysses (*Odyssey* XXI).[6]

The Clever Servant

We encounter the clever servant in an almost infinite variety of texts – and guises. He is the manager and manipulator of the action, the repository of secret knowledge, the intriguer. Since the time of Plautus, his task is to bring the lovers together and secure the happy end dictated by the genre of comedy – verisimilitude is not his concern. His qualities tend towards the Machiavellian in the sense elaborated by the author of *Il Principe* (1513) that a servant worth his salt can, by rendering himself indispensable, 'manage' his master.

In the era of the French Revolution of 1789 the clever literary servant becomes an apt vehicle of social satire. So revolutionary were the implications of Beaumarchais' comedy, *The Barber of Seville* (1784), and Denis Diderot's brilliantly witty philosophical novel, *Jacques le Fataliste* (1773–5), that neither could appear in print until after the 1789 Revolution. For here the servant reveals himself, not merely as cleverer than his master, but by that fact conveys a socially subversive message: wherein lies the legitimacy of the old regime if the servant is mentally or morally the real master?[7]

The Foolish Servant

The foolish servant serves his master according to his lights, often, and particularly in modern literature, more faithfully than his smarter colleague. As the recipient of frequent beatings, not all deserved, he provides pantomimic entertainment for the spectator. German literature in the era of the Enlightenment and early Romanticism provides novel insights into the relationship between reason and instinct in the person of the simple servant, and can even become a guide to the philosophical debates of the day.[8] Thus the central issue of Heinrich von Kleist's highly original adaptation of Plautus (and Molière's) comedy, *Amphitryon* (1807), is identity: of Jupiter and Amphitryon, and at a lower social level of the two servants Mercury and Sosias. The latter is incapable of understanding how Mercury could have stolen his identity. Who is he now? Is there in fact such a thing as personal identity? Does the 'subject' actually exist or are we all creatures of others' impressions? And yet, for all his slow wit, it is Sosias, not Mercury, who comes closest to the truth and hence to the moral implications of the god Jupiter's wicked deception of the innocent and faithful wife Alkmene.

Servant as Messenger

While the *servus callidus* remains the focus of writers' attention down to our own day, the third type, the servant as messenger, is potentially the most interesting, and certainly so in the present context. The messenger is the 'hand' of his master (or mistress), to deliver his or her command. He comes in unexpected forms, from the banal to the sublime, embracing both the self-important 'herald', the March hare in *Alice in Wonderland* and the Pre-Cursor himself, along with all the celestial and satanic messengers in the Bible and secular literary texts. He takes on a wholly new guise in the twentieth-century media, and in logical development of the idea of the messenger as identical with his 'mission', the medium in Marshal McLuhan's famous phrase, 'becomes' the message. But perhaps the original 'subversive' servants are to be found, not in secular comedy, but in Judaeo-Christian texts, beginning with the figure of the light bearer, known as Lucifer.

Lucifer – The Original 'Subversive' Servant

When the artist Pablo Picasso walked along the beach in his Catalan adoptive home and selected the rusting handlebars of a discarded racing bicycle to serve as centrepiece for a whole host of his late works, paintings, etchings, lithographs, in the form of the horns of a bull, he was seeing with the eyes of a child. He sought to 're-enter' Paradise by re-creating the child's imaginative world,

185

mediating between man and the created world, between civilisation and nature, reason and instinct, which for Christians the Fall, and for secular man the glorification of the rational, had destroyed. 'Let there be Light', ordained God on the first day of Creation (Gen I:1). The figure of Lucifer, servant of the Almighty, was thus accorded high station as one of the greatest of the angels. His challenge to the Almighty, based in pride, *superbia,* led to his being banished into the darkness. Lucifer destroyed the harmony of the cosmos and brought dualism into the world.

How Baroque painters of the mighty altar pieces of Counter-Reformation parish and monastic Churches loved to depict the drama of Lucifer's expulsion from heaven![9] Here God's agent or servant is the Archangel Michael, whose name means, 'he who is as God'. After the Fall, Lucifer becomes Satan, the Prince of Darkness, perpetually seeking vengeance on God by preying on his Creation, mankind. The image of Satan as a serpent underlines the hierarchy of things: man walks erect, the serpent crawls on his belly. Light comes from above, but danger from below. The Christian imagination adopts the notion of life's ideal journey as 'ascent' to Heaven, with 'descent' into Hell as its awful alternative.

No poet has captured with greater brilliance the Christian cosmos, nor indeed the sheer horror of Satan's power, than Dante in *The Divine Comedy.* The omnipresence of Satan is reflected in his many names.[10] In the New Testament we encounter him as Beelzebub, Lucifer and Satan. In *Inferno* Dante terms him Dis, luridly representing him as physically terrifying through his sheer size and repulsive in his covering of coarse hair, up which Dante, accompanied by Virgil, must climb. In the modern era Lucifer is aptly conveyed by the idea of mask, but in the Nietzschean sense – since the devil is negation, incapable of creating – without any substance behind.

Devils people the medieval stage and the morality plays of Tudor England. Usually they announce their presence in advance by loud and frightening noises (compare the 'fee-fi-fo-fum' of pantomine giants). Or, as in late medieval French *diableries,* they run amok in the audience, pinching and smacking, to remind the spectator of the ubiquity of evil. Restoration comedy indulged the vogue for devils, to meet the taste of that gloomy expert on demonology on the throne and avid witch-burner, James I of England. The idea of the devilish kingdom had been borrowed from Machiavelli in his fable of the devil Belfagor, *The devil who took a wife* (c.1513–7), which told the tale of the devil who sought refuge back in hell as a better option than living with his nagging wife on earth. By portraying the 'alternative' kingdom of Hell and rendering Satan and his minions comic, the authors, such as Ben Jonson in *The Diville is an Asse* (1616), were not trivialising evil. Rather they were subscribing to the idea that laughter can allay fear. Fear of Satan was very real in the early modern age, capable of being manipulated to promote the kind of mass hysteria that gave rise to the witch crazes, matched only in horror by twentieth-century holocausts.

Dante describes Lucifer as having been 'the fairest of the fairest sons of light' (*Inferno,* Canto 34:8). The fallen angel, God's subversive servant, embodies in the Christian tradition the idea of evil as the negation of all that is good and beautiful. As such he and his kind are represented as ugly to the point of physical repulsion. The grotesqueness of Satan's form, exemplified in satanic grimaces, is designed to elicit horror and fear of evil.

Enlightenment art and literature make a radical break with this tradition. A landmark figure in the evolution of the modern devil is Milton's Lucifer in *Paradise Lost.* Arguably, *Paradise Lost* is not in its essence a religious poem, for Milton's Lucifer begins the process of aestheticising evil, which leads to its 'taming' and ultimately to its denial. Milton's Lucifer is a man of great physical beauty. His challenge to the Deity reinforces the new perspective of man as the measure of all things. The coldness of the 'new' Satan, once associated with satanic denial of life and love, will in modern literature be rendered in psychological terms as a kind of existential loneliness, forcefully conveyed in Byron's epic poem *Cain* (1821).

Meanwhile the Faust legend, originating with the seminal text *Historia von D. Johann Faust* of 1587, and elaborated by Christopher Marlowe in his *Tragicall Historie of the Life and Death of Doctor Faustus* (1631), had begun to exercise its fascination over the European literary imagination. As late as 1947 in his novel of Hitler's Third Reich, *Dr Faustus,* Thomas Mann employed it as a mightily extended metaphor for the enslavement of a whole people.[11]

In Marlowe's and Goethe's Faust, the devil appears as the servant of Man. But what a world separates the two. Marlowe's Faustus, assisted, it is true, by Mephostophilis, makes the conscious choice which leads to his damnation. The example of his awful fate, acted out before them in the tradition of the medieval morality play, strikes horror into the spectators. In Goethe, the devil Mephisto, like the comic servant of old, is the master of entertainment, a *servus callidus*, but a loveable rogue. Mephisto's self-characterisation as the spirit of negation: *'Ich bin der Geist, der stets verneint'* (I am the spirit that ever denies) subverts by denial the centuries-old belief in, and fear of evil. The historic significance of Goethe's *Faust* lies in popularising the idea of devil as helpmate of man in overcoming his fear of eating of the Tree of Knowledge, and so adopting as the devise of modern man: *sapere aude* (dare to know). Negativity becomes the spur to human endeavour. God is assigned merely to the 'framework tale'. In the *Prologue in Heaven* He is debased, de-throned in Mephisto's blasphemous parlance: *Der Alte*, a decent old boy. Hell is nowhere to be seen.

In another seemingly trivial respect, namely in his deportment and movement, Mephisto is reminiscent of the omnipresence of the serpent in the Garden of Eden – 'my cousin' *(meine Muhme)*, as he facetiously puts it in conversation with God in the Prologue in heaven (v. 335), Mephisto's forebears terrified by their size and might; he by contrast is slender, quick and athletic in all his movements. Where his forebears threatened, he ingratiates. The back of this modern tempter, like that of the indispensable clever servant, is elastic, perpetually bent in (feigned) subjection, as he peddles his wares. Capitalist modes of production in the nineteenth century linked text and graphics, providing a new 'stage' for the devil. By its end he had been discovered by the advertising industry as an apt medium for enticing the public to part with their hard-earned money. Temptation, like Satan, is trivialised as a medium of entertainment. 'Treat yourself', he urges, reinforcing the modern age's trend towards self-centred individualism.

Modern advertisements for the chocolate bar KitKat provide a revealing example of changing social values. In Ireland in the late

1980s, a popular ad showed a small boy with an eight-section KitKat bar surrounded by eight eager friends. As he hands out the second last piece, it dawns on him with horror that he has miscalculated. Either he or the last friend must go without. In a brave gesture he hands over the last piece. The advertisement was replaced in late 1990s 'Celtic Tiger Ireland' with one showing a young woman eating the entire bar, exclaiming as she went, 'and yet another for me and me and me ...'

Whereas on the one hand, the trivialisation of evil so characteristic of the modern age is symbolised in the glorification of one of the seven deadly sins (covetousness) as 'retail therapy', the power of what Christians term the devil manifests itself in quite other but equally destructive ways. An ancient tradition associated with the devil, his melancholy, is transposed into human consciousness, manifesting itself as existential angst and various forms of psychological ills. Modern (nineteenth- and twentieth-century) literature and art appears dominated by a fascination of evil to a degree which elicited from Pope John Paul II the rhetorical question: has not the mirroring of all that is negative in the great variety of contemporary art become an end in itself, making of evil a source of pleasure, destruction and death a form of entertainment, resulting in cynicism and a disregard for human life?[12]

Service at the Heart of the 'Suffering Servant' Gospel

Lucifer's antipode comes in the form of the angelical messenger, Gabriel. The Archangel's message, and its reception, reverses the 'old' order. With the connivance of Adam, Eve's challenge to God's order brought about the fall of man. Paradoxically, surrender of self by Mary becomes a key element of man's redemption. The Archangel's visit to the young virgin does not deliver a divine command. Rather does it offer her a genuine choice. The divine gift of free will is honoured by God in Gabriel's message. Though 'troubled', Mary makes a conscious choice. Through her acceptance, echoed every day in the Angelus, the lowly 'handmaid of the Lord' becomes the Blessed of Creation, the glory of our race. In echoing the prophet Samuel's, 'Here I am Lord. I come to do your will' and assuming the metaphorical guise of the servant, she anticipates the life of her Son on earth.

Of the many references to service as lying at the heart of Christ's teaching and recorded in the New Testament, chapter 13 of the Gospel of John surely provides the most graphic representation. The symbolism of the washing of the feet articulates scenically Christ's admonishment to the sons of Zebedee contained in both Matthew and Mark. The upper room becomes a theatre with the stage on two levels, but one which subverts traditional images of divine majesty and power. A fresco from Carolingian times represented God's power in the form of a hand, *pars pro toto*. The hand of the lawgiver is outstretched to his people. But John the Evangelist describes Christ's hand as placed *at* and *below* the feet of His servants, as he performs the most servile task a man can do. We recall that the foot is also the instrument of forcible subjection, the symbol of conquest.[13] Other images reinforce the significance of the text: Christ *kneels* at the feet of his disciples, having first 'girded' himself with a towel, a symbol for one who must be led 'where he would not go'. The willing, studied subjection of master to servant carries a powerful message, for:

> [A]nyone who wants to become great among you must be your servant, and anyone who wants to be first among you must be slave to all. For the Son of Man himself did not come to be served but to serve, and to give his life as a ransom for many. (Mk 10:43-45)

Service lies at the heart of the gospel message and has informed Christian teaching, if not always Christian practice, throughout the centuries. The Pope traditionally styled himself not just as the servant of God, but *servus servorum Dei* (servant of the servants of God). Service of God and humankind is, as the biblical scholar Raymond E. Brown has shown, a defining feature of the episcopal as of the priestly calling.[14] One of the most powerful manifestations of the Church's capacity for self-renewal[15] is seen today in the vision and practice of her agents world-wide. We see this, for example, in the new understanding of overseas mission. In former times missionaries brought, besides the gospel tidings, 'civilisation' to native peoples. Today, as in common with the ideal and practice of Christian charities world-wide,[16] service to the people, and on their terms, is the centre and meaning of their calling. So too the *Compendium of the Social Doctrine of the Catholic Church* offers inspiration to laymen and -women and religious alike, but also makes quite explicit demands on all its members to define their allegiance in terms of service to the people of God.

Subversion of received certainties was always the potential role of the servant, in literature and in the history of the human race. In that 'magnificent sense of the inversion of values that comes from knowing God's will',[17] we recognise subversion's most evocative manifestation in the person of the Messiah and Redemptor as 'suffering Servant'.[18]

Notes

1. Cervantes provides a delightful example of the contrast between the capacity for abstract thought of the (highborn) master, Don Quixote de la Mancha, and the literal imagination of the typical servant Sancho Pansa. This is the scene where the latter tells of the shepherd who has to transport three hundred goats one at a time across the river. Sancho starts describing the event three hundred times and proves quite unable of grasping Don Quixote's point that there are other (and briefer) ways of conveying the same information.

2. Though, as in the Greek form Hermes suggests, Mercury also belongs to the third category.

3. Our computer, designed as our tool, can forget its 'status' and behave like some clever but recalcitrant servant.

4. Thus hermeneutics from 'Hermes', messenger of the gods.

5. The association of the servant with the body (and the master with mind or spirit) is enduring. The rehabilitation of the body in Enlightenment anthropology *('commercium mentis et corporis')* had far-reaching consequences for the metaphorical role of the servant figure in modern art.

6. Shakespeare's comic recreation of the old female family servant in the person of the nurse in *Romeo and Juliet* proved, for

rather different reasons, equally enduring in western literature, until Dickens, among others, re-invested her with her original virtues, as in the figure of Peggotty in *David Copperfield*.

7. With an even lighter touch, the much underestimated literary genius, P.G. Wodehouse, makes the same point with the figure of Jeeves.

8. This is reflected in Christian literature featuring servants, as in *Poor, good Maria, or the portrait of a perfect servant* (Freiburg i.Br., Herder, 1801-3), who proves to have a more acute, because intuitive understanding of social realities than her 'betters', providing a model of right conduct for the rest.

9. As in the Benedictine abbey of Metten near Passau on the banks of the Danube, where a mighty golden Archangel Michael on the peak of the façade is seen hurling a huge and grimacing black devil into the waves below.

10. See, for example, Jeffrey Burton Russell, *The Prince of Darkness: Radical Evil and the Power of Good in History* (London, Routledge, 1989), p. 43.

11. Mann's exploitation of the idea of Hitler as the Arch-Tempter, the wicked servant who becomes the brutal master, had already been anticipated by the Viennese critic, Karl Kraus. Eda Sagarra, 'Der Herr und sein Diener oder der Diener als Herr. Zur Geschichte eines europäischen Topos', in Konrad Feilchenfeldt et al. (eds), *Zwischen Aufklärung und Romantik. Neue Wege der Forschung* (Würzburg: Könighausen & Neumann, 2006), pp. 218–231, at 227.

12. In an arresting article on the representation of evil in (modern) literature: 'Die literarische Gestaltung des Bösen' in *Internationale katholische Zeitschrift COMMUNIO* 11 (1989), pp. 489–499, Wolfgang Frühwald, recently retired president of the Humboldt Foundation, answers the Pope's question in the affirmative. Modern literature is obsessed with evil, which, he argues (498ff), is related to the paradox at the heart of creative genius: the poet, Poietés, is as 'creator' in competition with the Almighty, the Pan-Creator. Such, then, is the power but also the danger of art.

13. The iconic representation of Our Lady crushing the serpent's

head, transposed by Baroque artists from Genesis 3:15, is
another such graphically imagined 'reversal'.

14. In his short study, *Priest and Bishop: Biblical Reflections*
(London: Jeffrey Chapman, 1971), especially pp. 28–34.

15. 'Subversion' has always operated in the dynamic of threat/
chaos (as in the Roman Saturnalia) vs. hope/renewal and rebirth.

16. As, for example, for the Society of St Vincent de Paul in John-
Mark McCafferty, 'What kind of "Society" do we want?' The
Irish SVP *Ozanam Bulletin,* Summer 2007, pp. 28f.

17. Brown (op.cit.), p. 31.

18. *Catechism of the Catholic Church,* n. 615 (London: Jeoffrey
Chapman, 1999), p. 140.

19   *In the World but Not of It*

Dr David Stevens

C hristian faith challenges all exclusive claims of tribe, tradition and political commitment. The gospel invites us into the space created by Christ and to find there those who were previously our enemies. It therefore seeks to break down the enmity between us; enmity caused by different traditions and national, political and religious loyalties. The gospel opens up for us a view of wholeness, justice and living in right relations, which sees the whole world as potential brothers and sisters – a nourishing and fulfilment of the human. This is a vision of a new humanity reconciled in Christ and living together in a new community.

Through Christ a new relationship is established between those who accept the gift of reconciliation – strangers become citizens and aliens are recognised as members of the household of God (Eph 2:19). These redeemed people are called to be a community of reconciliation – a community of openness and inclusion – united round the excluded One, Jesus Christ, who has been raised by God. In this they seek to reflect the strangeness, unlikeness and surprising nature of the faith that Jesus brought. Because this community is formed around the excluded One, its paradigmatic activity is the practice of hospitality and welcome of the stranger – the person who is always in danger of exclusion. We know that the reality of the Church is not usually like this. Yet what has happened in history is the introduction of a glimpse of a radically different world – a peaceable kingdom not structured by violence and the exclusion and sacrificial practices of the world. And there continues to be glimpses.

However, the reality – the sociological reality – is that Churches are part of communities and nations; they cannot be Other. They are chaplains, reflectors, consciences, restrainers, discerners, givers of wisdom, custodians of collective memory and places of community belonging. Churches bring 'their' community before God. They are places where the 'specialness' and stories of communities can be celebrated. But 'specialness' can lead to exclusivity and a sense of superiority. Churches can be places where we are told – implicitly and explicitly – who does not belong to our community: by who is prayed for and who is not; by the contents of sermons and by the symbols displayed or not displayed. Thus Churches are often excluding and exclusive.

As a reality in the world, a church is a home for the community or the nation, governed by the social 'other' that often brings rivalry, violence, scapegoating and sacrificial outcomes. And it is a 'temple' providing a place of customary ritual for the community and the nation so that 'normal' life, with all its ambiguity, can go on. And at the same time it lives by a story of a Jesus who died outside the camp (Heb 13:13) and who, while completely a Jew, did not belong to his world (Jn 17:14) and so was driven out of it by those who did not want to be disturbed by another way. All our 'homes' – personal, communal, national – are radically de-centred by Jesus, 'For there is no eternal city for us in this life. But we look for one in the life to come' (Heb 13:14). All the gospels bear witness to Jesus subverting the Temple from within. And the Church is a community where Jew and Greek, bound and free, belong (Cor 12:13); in its very essence it transcends all social, cultural and national boundaries. Churches constantly backslide from the knowledge given in and through Jesus Christ, to one given by their social reality (which includes politics, culture, national and ethnic identity). Thus Churches live in a contradiction, which is manifested in living in a tension: in the world, but not of it (cf Jn 18:36). The danger is that in situations of communal conflict the tension collapses and, as the Croatian theologian Miroslav Volf says:

Churches often find themselves accomplices in war rather than agents of peace. We find it difficult to distance ourselves from our own culture so we echo its reigning opinions and mimic its practices.[1]

They provide ideological ammunition to protect the kingdoms of this world (cf Jn 18:36).

The Janus Face of Religion

Religion plays a profoundly ambiguous role in conflict situations. On the one hand it can encourage hatred – anti-Catholicism is particularly potent in Northern Ireland – and has political consequences. Churches can reinforce community division and harden boundaries; Catholic views and rules on mixed marriage and the importance of Church schools have had significant consequences in Northern Irish society. Religion can give divine sanction to nationalism, political positions and violence. Shimon Peres, President of Israel, says of Hezbollah, the Lebanese Shiite terrorist group: 'These are religious people. With the religious you can hardly negotiate. They think they have supreme permission to kill people and go to war. This is their nature'.[2] Jihadist groups pursue holy war and see suicide bombing as a religious act. In conflict situations theologies of enmity, superiority and distorted recognition of others can easily gain prominence, for example, the Dutch Reformed Church in South Africa theologically legitimated apartheid. When Churches and religions find themselves on different sides of a fear-threat relationship between two communities, there can be a political/religious symbiosis, for example, in Northern Ireland there was Protestantism/unionism and Catholicism/nationalism.

Churches find it difficult to establish any critical distance from the pressures coming from 'their' community. The temptation is to identify without reserve and to become chaplains to 'their' community. Ian Linden has written about the 'stranglehold that ethnicity had gained' in the Church in Rwanda. The Church 'had never seriously challenged Hutu to Tutsi identity as potentially open to being re-imagined in a Christian form, because ethnicity had always been taken as a given'.[3] When the genocide occurred in 1994, the Church found it very difficult to resist the dynamics of hatred and killing. There were a significant number of prominent Christians involved in the killings (although there were Church people who resisted and were martyred). In the former Yugoslavia, some Churches became guardians of national identity. There was a religious/national symbiosis and some people who committed war crimes regarded themselves as defending not only their nation, but their faith as well.

On the other hand, religion can be a force for restraint and this has been generally true in Northern Ireland. Without the Churches the situation would have been worse. The preaching and living out of non-retaliation, forbearance and forgiveness have had real positive social consequences. The Churches opposed those who espoused violence and the gods of nationalism. Churches working together have been a force for good, they have helped lessen the religious/ political symbiosis. The developing pattern of Church leaders and others meeting together over the last thirty years in Northern Ireland – for instance, through the Irish Inter-Church Meeting[4] – and of clergy visiting victims of violence together, has been a significant public witness. Churches have been encouragers to politicians seeking political compromise. There have been many individuals and groups, for example, Corrymeela, working for peace and reconciliation.

Contacts were established by Church groups with paramilitary organisations; clergy and others acted as go-betweens. The Irish Council of Churches, together with the Roman Catholic Church, have had a peace education programme working in schools, and so on. And, nevertheless, the picture is very mixed and deeply ambiguous – some black, much grey, a little white. Churches are part of the problem and struggle to be part of the solution.[5]

The Church in Fiji illustrates this well. During the coup in 1987 by the military, many of the instigators were deeply steeped in Christian religious practice who openly invoked their faith as a guide for their action:

The temptation was strong to align the church to the interests of chauvinist politicians who seized control of the State and sought legitimation of their rule that pitched one ethnic community against another. It fell upon another set of church leaders to defy the military and secular authorities in advocating an alternative course of reconciliation.[6]

In the former Yugoslavia, after peace was declared, religious institutions and communities by and large found themselves appealing for forgiveness in their general statements but not being able to stop blaming and judging each other.

The problem is that politics appears to dominate the Churches more than vice versa. This is one very significant factor in inhibiting Churches in being agents of co-operation, and it raises profound questions about what is more important: religious commitment or political commitment. In theological terms, we are talking about the issue of idolatry.

Churches tend to reflect people's fears, reflect community divisions, reflect a community experience of violence and threat, rather than act as agents of change or transformers of conflict. Thus the Protestant Church in Northern Ireland often talked about law and order, reflecting a community under siege, and the Catholic Church often talked about justice reflecting a community feeling of victimisation. However, Churches not only reflect people's fears, they can also amplify them (witness the role of the Rev. Dr Ian Paisley in Northern Ireland until recently).

Local Churches, in particular, often reflect people's sense of fear and threat. They are places of ordered calm – a safe space – where we are among our own. Our enemies are outside. They are 'protective fortresses for threatened people'[7] in the words of the political scientist Duncan Morrow, speaking of some Protestant Churches in Northern Ireland. Or they may be places that assume a symbiosis between religion and national identity, for example, Catholicism and Irishness. The prayers, the liturgy, the sermon, plaques and flags tell us who is outside and inside of our concern, who our enemies are, what state we belong to, often in highly oblique and coded ways. And, of course, in some settings a local

Church may also contain a lot of political difference within it. Then the rule tends to be that these differences are never talked about, but we all know they are there. And because they are never talked about they can never be dealt with. Clergy in such contexts find themselves in a very unfree and very vulnerable position.

Positive Deviants

In divided societies, fear, anxiety and a sense of threat are encoded. They almost become part of people's genetic make-up. As the dynamics of conflict gather force, individuals and groups disappear into a vortex of antagonism. They are magnetised by violence. It takes very strong people to stand out when all around succumb, and it is true that some people can stand outside the vortex of antagonism. In Northern Ireland some Church people are the most committed in terms of peace and reconciliation, common witness and co-operation, and have been so since the start of the Troubles. In Rwanda, some Christians were martyred for standing against the ethnic hatred and killing. In Fiji, some Christian leaders resisted the coup and stood for reconciliation between ethnic groups. It is these 'exceptions' that are the really interesting people, because they tell us about a kingdom that is not of this world (Jn 18:36) and of a Church that is called to be a witness to this kingdom. The marks of this kingdom are people who are 'different and strange' – positive deviants are:

- Able to stand out against community hatred;
- Able to cross community boundaries;
- Able to be peacemakers;
- Able to be healers;
- Able to forgive;
- Able to stand with the victims;
- Able to engage in costly action;
- Able to be witnesses to truth.

When we see this 'difference' and 'strangeness'[8] we are in the presence of 'transcendence-in-the-midst'[9] and in the presence of witness to the Kingdom of God. The message of reconciliation is

199

made visible and we learn what humanity might be – the church exists for this purpose.

I am a member of a community of reconciliation in Northern Ireland, the Corrymeela Community. Corrymeela has worked, often residentially, with a huge mixture of people from all sorts of backgrounds. We have been journeying together for over forty years and there are 'graduates' of Corrymeela all over the place. During that time we have learnt the importance of:

- Belonging together in a community of diversity;
- Reconciliation being a practice and a journey, not a theory or a strategy or a technique;
- A safe space where people can come and meet each other, where there is an atmosphere of trust and acceptance and where differences can be acknowledged, explored and accepted;
- Presence and accompaniment of people who can give time and attention;
- A community of faith being able to bring healing, of being a 'touching place';
- Encounter and relationships: it is only in encounter and relationships that words like trust, reconciliation and forgiveness become real;
- Acknowledging and sharing vulnerability;
- People telling their stories and listening to other people's stories. Our identities and lives are based strongly on the stories we tell about ourselves, our families, our communities and our countries. Thus we need places where memories are explored and untangled;
- Not writing people off as incorrigible 'baddies' no matter what they have done – this is not to trivialise evil or say wrong does not matter;
- The avoidance of self-righteousness and an awareness of our own hypocrisy;
- Surprise and the unexpected: reconciliation is something given as well as a practice;
- Taking small steps;

- Being sustained and nourished by hope and a vision of a different future;
- Being involved for the long haul;
- A recognition that the transformation of the world is linked to the transformation of ourselves.

At their centre, Churches have a narrative of forgiveness, reconciliation, new possibilities and new identities which, if it was really believed and acted on, could be transforming. The challenge is to believe and act.

Notes

1. Volf, M., 'A Vision of Embrace: Theological Perspectives on Cultural Identity and Conflict', *Ecumenical Review,* Vol. 47 (1995/2), p. 200.
2. *The New Yorker* (New York), October 14 and 21, 2002, p. 195.
3. Linden, Ian, 'The Church and Genocide: Lessons from the Rwandan Tragedy' in Gregory Baum and Harold Wells (eds), *The Reconciliation of Peoples: Challenges to the Churches* (Geneva: WCC, 1997), p. 52.
4. A special report on religion and public life in *The Economist,* November 3–9, 2007, says of Ireland, 'The cycle of violence that Cromwell did so much to create lasted for over 300 years. Eventually sectarianism covered a tangle of other ideas ... The beginning of the end began to come when preachers from both sides of the divide began to condemn violence ... In most parts of the world that is yet to come.' This is a very interesting suggestion that something changed in Ireland and it changed in the religious world first. And, of course, as the quotation suggests, it is the tangle of religion with other things – economics, culture, politics, colonisation – that is the potent thing. Change in the realm of religion may lead to change in other areas of life. Certainly it is true that Protestant and Catholic Church-people engaged long before the politicians.
5. As part of a society dealing with the past, the Churches need to critically examine – separately and together – their role in the Troubles. Churches are in the business of acknowledgement

and repentance, not avoidance and evasion, which seems to be the preferred societal and political mode of dealing with the past at present, plus, of course, blaming religion and the Churches.

6. Premdas, Ralph R., 'The Church and Reconciliation in Ethnic Conflicts: The Case of Fiji', in Baum and Wells (eds), *The Reconciliation of Peoples,* p. 93.

7. Morrow, Duncan, Birrell, Derek, Greer, John and O'Keefe, Terry, *The Churches and Inter-Community Relationships* (Coleraine: University of Ulster, 1994), p. 261.

8. The Jewish philosopher Emmanuel Levinas speaks of God in terms of that which is 'different and strange'.

9. See David Jenkin's *The Contradiction of Christianity* (London: SCM, 1976).

GLOSSARY OF ABBREVIATIONS

CPCE	Community of Protestant Churches in Europe
CEC	Conference of European Churches
PCPCU	Pontifical Council for the Promotion of Christian Unity
WARC	World Alliance of Reformed Churches
CTBI	Churches Together in Britain and Ireland
WCC	World Council of Churches
IARCCUM	International Anglican Roman Catholic Commission for Unity and Mission
ARCIC	Anglican–Roman Catholic International Commission
EBE	European Baptist Federation
ROCOR	Russian Orthodox Church Outside of Russia
CELAM	Catholic Bishops' Conference of Latin America
DCC	Dublin Council of Churches
ICC	Irish Council of Churches
GCP	Global Christian Forum
CUV	Common Understanding and Vision of the World Council of Churches
SACC	South African Council of Churches
CS/CWCs	Conference of Secretaries of Christian World Communions
CCA	Christian Conference of Asia
FABC	(Catholic) Federation of Asian Bishops' Conferences
AACC	All Africa Conference of Churches
AEA	Association of Evangelicals in Africa
EFA	Evangelical Fellowship of Asia
ERCDOM	Evangelical–Roman Catholic Dialogue on Mission
OAIC	Organisation of African Instituted Churches
GTUN	Growing Together in Unity and Mission
ECUSA	Episcopal Church of the United States of America
IICM	Irish Inter-Church Meeting
PACE	Protestant and Catholic Encounter